LAD = 10/29/94/
C = 11
SJPL = 6
4/96

RELIGION

A REFERENCE FIRST BOOK

BY GILDA BERGER
DRAWINGS BY
ANNE CANEVARI GREEN

X291.0321

9/83

FRANKLIN WATTS
NEW YORK | LONDON | TORONTO
SYDNEY | 1983

Photographs courtesy of
the Religious News Service:
pp. 7, 25, 54, 58 (top and bottom),
66, 67, 73, 75, and 78;
the New York Public Library Picture Collection:
pp. 13, 17, 22, 26, 28, 39,
43, 50, 53, 74, 90, and 94.

Library of Congress Cataloging in Publication Data

Berger, Gilda.
Religion.

(A Reference first book)
Summary: A lexicon of the world's religions,
religious movements, and religious leaders, including
information on scriptures and forms of worship.
1. Religions—Dictionaries, Juvenile.
[1. Religions—Dictionaries]
I. Green, Anne Canevari, ill.   II. Title.   III. Series.
BL92.B47 1983   291'.03'21   82-17651
ISBN 0-531-04538-2

RELIGION

ABRAHAM. Known principally as the founder of Judaism. Moslems also consider Abraham their ancestor, through his son Ishmael.

The Hebrew Bible reports that Abraham was born in the city of Ur in the Chaldees, where people believed in many gods. God revealed himself to Abraham and told him that he would found a great nation. He instructed Abraham to journey to Canaan. Abraham sought and eventually found the new land, holding to his belief that there was only one God, the creator and ruler of all.

God tested Abraham's devotion by asking him to sacrifice his beloved son Isaac. Abraham's willingness to take this step, though at the last moment God withdrew the request, often serves as an example of dedication to God of the highest order.

The Bible reports that God made a covenant, or agreement, with Abraham. He promised to Abraham all the land of Canaan for his people and for the descendants of his son Isaac. *See also* ISAAC; ISHMAEL; and JUDAISM.

AGNOSTIC. Someone who believes that knowledge of the existence of God, the purpose of life, and even what is real and what is not real are unknown and unknowable. The word comes from a Greek word, *agnostos*, which means "unknown" or "unknowable." The scientist Thomas Henry Huxley, who held this belief, may have been the first to use the word in its present meaning, in 1869.

ALLAH. The name of the Supreme Being in the religion of Islam. The word is Arabic and is made up of *al* (''the'') and *ilah* (''God''). According to Islamic writings, ''There is no God but Allah, and Mohammed is the Apostle of Allah.'' *See also* ISLAM.

ALL SAINTS' DAY. A Christian holiday observed on November 1 each year, mostly to honor the Christian saints who do not have days named for them. All Saints' Day was first celebrated on November 1, 608. ''Allhallows Eve,'' better known as Halloween, comes on October 31, the night before All Saints' Day.

ALTAR. A raised place used in religious worship. Ancient peoples sacrificed animals or even humans at altars. Christians use the altar to perform such ceremonies as the Holy Eucharist. Sometimes incense is burned. Worshipers in other religions bring offerings or kneel before the altar of a favorite god.

ANGEL. A spiritual or heavenly creature who acts as God's servant and messenger. The name comes from the Greek word *angelos*, which means ''messenger.'' Angels are usually shown as beings with human bodies and wings.

Several religions rank angels just below God and just above humans. In the traditional hierarchy, however, there are nine levels of angels. In descending order these are: seraphim, cherubim, thrones, dominions, virtues, powers, principalities, archangels, and angels. Angels who rebelled against this order are the so-called ''fallen angels.'' Satan, or the devil, the ruler of hell, is a fallen angel. *See also* DEVIL.

ANGLICAN. *See* CHURCH OF ENGLAND.

ANIMISM. A belief that everything in nature, even a lifeless object such as a stone, has a spirit. Animists try to please the spirits so that they will not do harm.

ANNUNCIATION. In the Christian religion, the revelation brought to the Virgin Mary by the angel Gabriel that Mary had been chosen to be the mother of Jesus, the son of God.

The words of the Annunciation, ''Hail Mary, full of grace, the Lord is with thee,'' later became the opening words of the ''Hail Mary'' prayer.

Many artists have created paintings of the Annunciation. Most show Mary holding a book or some embroidery, while Gabriel carries an olive branch or a flower. *See also* VIRGIN MARY.

This painting of the Annunciation, which hangs in the Vatican Museum, is by artist Giuseppe Cesari.

APOSTLES. The twelve men whom Jesus chose to spread his ideas. The apostles included Saint Andrew, Saint Bartholomew, Saint James, Saint John the Evangelist, Judas Iscariot, Saint Jude, Saint Matthew, Saint Matthias, Saint Peter, Saint Philip of Bethsaida, Saint Simon the Canaanite, and Saint Thomas.

AQUINAS, SAINT THOMAS (1225?–1274). A major theologian of the Roman Catholic Church. Aquinas was born in Italy. His writings combined Aristotle's thought with Christian revelation. He showed that there is no conflict between the principles of philosophy and the beliefs of Christianity.

ARCHBISHOP. In the Roman Catholic, Eastern Orthodox, and Anglican churches, the bishop in charge of a particular province.

The archbishop controls a number of districts, or dioceses, within the province, each headed by a bishop. The archbishop has religious authority over all the bishops of his ''archdiocese,'' although he does not usually become involved in local church affairs.

The pope is the archbishop of Rome. He appoints the Roman Catholic archbishops and gives them a *pallium*—a vestment, or robe that symbolizes their position. The archbishop of Canterbury is the head of the Church of England. *See also* BISHOP.

ASCENSION DAY. *See* HOLY THURSDAY.

ASH WEDNESDAY. The first day of Lent. The holiday is observed by Roman Catholic churches, the Church of England, the Protestant Episcopal Church, and some other Protestant churches in America. *See also* LENT.

ATHEIST. Someone who does not believe in the existence of God. The doctrine that says there is no God is called atheism.

BAHAISM. A religion stemming from the Shiite branch of the Islamic religion and seeking world unity. Bahaism was founded in the mid-nineteenth century by Bahaullah and was based on the teachings of Bab-ud-Din.

The fundamental idea of the Baha'i faith is that despite the many differences among the world's religions, they are all one. There is but one faith and one evolving truth, which should guide every individual in worship and every society in its laws and customs.

Followers of the Baha'i faith hold that God can only be known through his acts and divine revelation, which are continual and ever-changing. The message of God has come to earth through a number of prophets—Abraham, Moses, Jesus, Buddha, Mohammed, Bab-ud-Din ("Gate of the Faith"), and finally, Bahaullah ("Glory of Allah").

In the 1840s, Bab-ud-Din (1819–1850) preached the coming of a new prophet to Persia (now Iran). He was executed in 1850 by the Persian officials of Islam for his heretical beliefs. His work was carried forward by Bahaullah (1817–1892), who was accepted as the prophet described by Bab-ud-Din and who organized the Baha'i faith.

Although they suffered from persecution by the Islamic governments of Persia and elsewhere, the followers of Baha'i grew in numbers, especially in the early years of the twentieth century. Today there are about 100,000 Baha'is in the United States and 5 million worldwide. The central Baha'i house of worship is in Haifa, Israel. The main center in the United States is in Wilmette, Illinois. *See also* BAHAULLAH.

BAHAULLAH (1817–1892). Founder of the Baha'i faith. Bahaullah was born in Persia (now Iran) and was the son of a wealthy official. He was originally named Husayn Ali. His changed name, Bahaullah, means ''Glory of Allah.''

In the 1840s, Bahaullah joined a group led by Bab-ud-Din, who was preaching the unity of the world and all its religions. As Bahaullah spread Bab-ud-Din's message, he was exiled and later imprisoned. Despite these difficulties, he continued his work. In time, he gained recognition as a prophet and, partly because of the writings he left behind, became the central figure in the emerging religion of Baha'i.

BAPTISM. A ceremony used to mark a person's entry into the Christian religion. Its origin is uncertain but probably goes back to a Jewish ritual.

Early Christians were completely submerged in water for their baptism. Some modern baptisms, such as those practiced by Baptists, require submersion; but most just involve sprinkling water on the head.

John the Baptist performed the baptism ceremony for Jesus. Jesus then commanded his followers, ''Go ye therefore and teach all nations, baptizing them in the name of the Father, and of the Son, and of the Holy Ghost.''

Baptism can occur at almost any time in a person's life. Sometimes the baptism of an infant is known as a christening. At this occasion the child is named and formally inducted into the religion. Godparents may be present to promise to raise the child as Christian if the parents are not able to do so.

BAPTISTS. Members of a worldwide Protestant Christian sect, which has its greatest membership in the United States.

One of the most central Baptist beliefs is that of baptism by complete immersion in water for adult believers. Baptists do not practice infant baptism. In general, they derive their principles from the Christian Bible and believe in the freedom of each person to interpret the sacred writings as he or she sees fit.

The forerunners of the Baptist Church appeared in the sixteenth century when several religious leaders spoke out against infant baptism, claiming it went against the teachings of the New Testament. The person usually credited with founding the modern Baptist Church is John Smyth (1570–1612). Smyth was born in England. A vicar and preacher in the Church of England, Smyth later became involved in the English Separatist movement and fled to Amsterdam in 1608. Two years later he founded a church by baptizing first himself and then others. Some members of his church returned to England and established similar churches there. The first such church in America was organized in Providence, Rhode Island, in 1639 by Roger Williams. By 1644 the term Baptist Church was the common name taken by these groups.

Today, a number of different Baptist organizations exist in the United States. The total membership exceeds 25 million. *See also* BAPTISM.

BAR MITZVAH. A ceremony that takes place on a Sabbath (Saturday) near a Jewish boy's thirteenth birthday. After much study and preparation, the boy reads aloud a portion of the Torah at the morning service. He then becomes *bar mitzvah*, a ''son of the commandment.'' After this, he is considered a full member of the congregation and assumes all the religious duties of an adult man. *See also* TORAH.

BAS MITZVAH. A Jewish confirmation ceremony for girls who are around the age of thirteen. It is similar to the service for boys called a bar mitzvah. *Bas mitzvah* means ''daughter of the commandment.'' The ceremony is observed in Conservative and Reform Judaism but is not part of Orthodox Judaism. Also called bat mitzvah. *See also* BAR MITZVAH.

BHAGAVAD-GITA. A sacred work of Hinduism that interprets the religion. *See also* HINDUISM.

BIBLE. A collection of sacred writings used by both Jews and Christians. The word *bible* comes from the Greek word *biblia*, meaning ''books.''

The Hebrew Bible contains the history of the Jews and their code of laws. It is divided into three parts. The first part, called the Law, also called the Torah or Pentateuch, includes five books—Genesis, Exodus, Leviticus, Numbers, and Deuteronomy. Tradition holds that Moses wrote this portion of the Bible. The second part, Prophets, is the largest, with twenty-one separate books that range from Joshua and Judges to Zechariah and Malachi. The final part is called the Writings. Psalms, Proverbs, Job, Ecclesiastes, Esther, and Daniel are among the books found here.

The Christian Bible consists of sixty-six separate books (eighty-one in the Roman Catholic Bible) divided into two main sections, the Old Testament (which is the Hebrew Bible) and the New Testament. The New Testament contains twenty-seven books divided into three main groups. The first section is made up of the four Gospels—Matthew, Mark, Luke, and John—which are accounts of the life of Jesus—and the acts of the twelve apostles. In the second section are found the twenty-one Epistles, or letters, some of which are known by the name of the person addressed, others of which are known by the name of the author. The final section has only one book, Revelation, also called Apocalypse.

Scholars believe that the Hebrew and Christian Bibles were written by many authors. The Hebrew Bible was written over a period of a thousand years, the New Testament over a period of about ninety years. Since then, there have been many different translations and editions. One of the best-known editions of the Christian Bible was printed by Johannes Gutenberg in 1456. It was one of the first books to be printed using movable type.

BISHOP. For the Roman Catholic, Eastern Orthodox, and Anglican churches, the spiritual and religious leader of a district or diocese. The bishop's power is based on a belief in the succession of the apostles. In other words, the bishops hold office through an unbroken line that dates back to the time when Saint Peter was the first bishop of Rome (A.D. 42–67). The traditional symbols of a bishop of the Roman Catholic Church are a crosier, or shepherd's staff, and a miter, which is a tall hat shaped like an arch.

BOOTH, WILLIAM (1829–1912). An English religious leader and founder of the Salvation Army. In 1852, William Booth became a minister in the Methodist Church. But by 1865, he had started his own independent religious sect. In 1878, the Christian mission at Whitechapel, London, which he had organized, became the Salvation Army. *See also* SALVATION ARMY.

BRAHMA. One of the three aspects of God in the Hindu religion. Brahma is known as the Creator of the Universe and is considered a remote, impersonal god, difficult to approach. *See also* BRAHMAN and HINDUISM.

BRAHMAN. The Supreme Being, or World Spirit, in the Hindu religion. This spirit has no gender and is serene, impersonal, and without beginning or end. It is present in all of nature and in the human soul, reason, and will. Through proper discipline, Hindus strive to become one with the World Soul of Brahman.

Brahman is thought to be three gods in one. As the god Brahma, Brahman is the Creator of the World. As Vishnu, Brahman is the Preserver. And as Siva, Brahman is the Destroyer.

The Upanishads, which were written about 800 B.C., present the concept of Brahman. According to this set of sacred writings, salvation can be achieved through religious observances and speculation on the Supreme Being. *See also* BRAHMA; HINDUISM; SIVA; UPANISHADS; and VISHNU.

BUDDHA. (563?–483 B.C.). The title given to a man named Siddhartha Gautama who lived in India and laid the foundation for the religion of Buddhism. Buddha's followers call him Gautama Buddha. *Buddha* means ''Enlightened One'' in the Sanskrit language.

Seated Buddha.
This sandstone sculpture is
from the eighth century A.D.

Little is known about the life of Buddha. We do know that his family was well-to-do and reared him as a prince. He was completely shut away from the troubles of the world.

At age twenty-nine, he saw suffering for the first time. The knowledge that all people become sick and old and eventually die greatly disturbed him. He decided to give up his inheritance and leave his family and the luxuries of court life in order to find the cause of suffering in the world. This is called the Great Renunciation.

For six years, Gautama lived the life of a holy man. He practiced yoga, fasted, and lived as a hermit. But this brought him no understanding. Then, while meditating under a wild fig tree, now called the bo tree (Tree of Wisdom), a solution came to him. Buddhists know this as The Enlightenment. Simply put, it was that each person could attain nirvana by gaining a knowledge of one's self through spiritual discipline and by taking the ''middle way'' between a life of self-indulgence and a life of austerity.

Over the next forty-five years, Buddha practiced the Four Noble Truths and the Eight-Fold Path to peace and salvation. His disciples set up various orders of monks and nuns who followed the strict rules of their communities and carried Buddha's message throughout India and into Tibet, Ceylon (now called Sri Lanka), Burma, and Thailand. Buddhism most differs from Hinduism in that it opposes worship, ceremony, priests, caste, and the idea of a supreme being.

At the age of eighty, the Buddha fell sick and died. His followers believe that he passed on to nirvana. *See also* BUDDHISM; HINDUISM; and YOGA.

BUDDHISM. A religion that was started in India about 2,500 years ago by Gautama Buddha. Buddhism later spread to China, Japan, and other countries in Asia. After the seventh century A.D., Buddhism steadily declined in India, all but disappearing from that country. There are, though, an estimated 5 million Buddhists in the Orient and in other parts of the world today, and there has been a resurgence of Buddhism in India in this century.

The basic belief of Buddhism is that life is full of suffering caused by desire. The way to end suffering and find peace is through the destruction of one's desires. Freedom from desire brings enlightenment and an end to the chain of births, deaths, and rebirths.

Central to the teachings of Buddhism are the Four Noble Truths and the Eight-Fold Path. The Four Noble Truths are: (1) Suffering is part of life. (2) The cause of suffering is the craving or selfish desire for things. (3) The cure for sorrow and suffering is the destruction of selfishness. (4) The way to crush selfishness is to follow the Eight-Fold Path.

The steps of the Eight-Fold Path are: (1) Accepting the Four Noble Truths (right belief). (2) Thinking in the right way, which leads you to help others (right aspiration). (3) Being kind in speech, avoiding boasting, gossip, and lies (right speech). (4) Doing what is right (right action). (5) Earning your living in a way that is thought good (right means of livelihood). (6) Avoiding evil thoughts and actions and working hard (right effort). (7) Learning to concentrate (right thought). (8) Being at peace in your mind (right meditation).

The symbol of Buddhism is the wheel, whose eight spokes represent the paths to nirvana. Nirvana is the blissful state, realized by Buddha, in which all suffering ends, and the soul joins the World Soul. Only those who gain perfect self-control, unselfishness, and complete knowledge can achieve nirvana.

After Gautama's death his followers formed into two basic groups, called Theravada Buddhists and Mahayana Buddhists. The Theravada form of the religion is followed mostly by southern Asians who live in Burma, Cambodia (now called Kampuchea), Sri Lanka, Laos, Thailand, and Vietnam. This group follows most closely Buddha's rules of conduct and stresses self-discipline as the way to find salvation.

Mahayana is also called the Northern Way. It is the chief faith of China, Japan, Korea, and Mongolia. In Tibet, a form of Mahayana called Lamaism is practiced. Mahayana believes that Buddha was a savior and that people can find salvation through faith.

The spread of Buddhism began after the death of Gautama around 483 B.C. It soon became the major faith of the people of India. Around 250 B.C., Buddhist missionaries brought the religion to Ceylon (now called Sri Lanka). Around the first century A.D., Buddhism arrived in China. In the 400s, the religion became established in Korea. The 500s saw the spread of Buddhism to Burma, Thailand, Kampuchea, and Japan.

The sacred scripture of Theravada Buddhism is the Tripitaka, meaning "Three Baskets." It was completed about four hundred years after Gautama's death. The Tripitaka contains the sayings of Buddha and rules for disciples. The original writings are preserved in Pali, the dialect spoken by Gautama and his followers. Mahayani Buddhists added other sections, the so-called Paradise Scriptures, which are preserved in Sanskrit. *See also* BUDDHA; HINDUISM; and ZEN.

CALIPH. The title of the successors of Mohammed, founder of the religion of Islam. The caliphs were leaders of the Moslems, or Islamic people, but not prophets. The first caliph, Abu Bakr, was chosen upon Mohammed's death. A caliph had to be a free adult male, of sound mind and body, of the Islamic faith, and familiar with Islamic law. The office of caliph was ended in 1924, during the Turkish Revolution. *See also* ISLAM and MOHAMMED.

CALVIN, JOHN (1509–1564). One of the leaders of the Protestant Reformation in Europe in the sixteenth century.

Calvin was born and educated in France. In 1532, he separated himself from the Roman Catholic Church and openly declared his acceptance of the ideas of Martin Luther. In 1533 he had to take refuge in Switzerland. While in exile, he wrote *Institutes of the Christian Religion*, a work that presented and defended some of the basic principles of Protestantism.

Calvinism started in Switzerland and spread through other parts of Europe. In Scotland, Calvin's principles inspired John Knox to lead the Scottish Protestant Reformation. The followers of Calvin broke with the Lutheran sect in 1561. Calvin's ideas were most influential in the formation of the Presbyterian Church. *See also* LUTHERANS; PREDESTINATION; PRESBYTERIANS; PROTESTANTISM; and REFORMATION.

CARDINAL. A leader of the Roman Catholic Church, just below the pope in rank. One hundred and twenty cardinals, all appointed by the pope, make up the Sacred College of Cardinals. They help the pope administer church affairs. On the death of a pope, the Sacred College elects the next pope, usually one of its own members. Among the symbols of the cardinal's office are the red *biretta,* or cap; the red cassock, or long outer robe; the red broad-brimmed hat and tassel; and a sapphire ring.

CASTE. *See* HINDUISM.

CATECHISM. A series of questions and answers used for teaching the Christian religion to children. It is also used with adults who are new to Christianity. The earliest catechisms date back to the eighth century A.D. Important Roman Catholic catechisms were issued in 1556 and 1566. Martin Luther prepared catechisms for Lutherans in 1520 and 1529.

CATHEDRAL. A Christian church at which a bishop presides. A number of glorious cathedrals were built in Europe during the Gothic period of architecture, from the twelfth through the fifteenth centuries. A few of the better-known are Chartres and Notre Dame in France and Canterbury and Westminster Abbey in England. *See also* CHURCH.

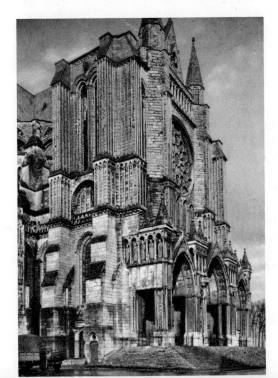

**The cathedral
at Chartres, France**

CATHOLICISM. *See* ROMAN CATHOLICISM.

CHAPLAIN. A member of the clergy. Chaplains conduct religious services in the armed forces or in institutions such as prisons and hospitals. In the United States, most chaplains are either Catholic priests, Jewish rabbis, or Protestant ministers.

CHRIST. The title of the savior within the Christian religion. *See also* JESUS.

CHRISTENING. *See* BAPTISM.

CHRISTIANITY. The religion that is based on the belief that Jesus is the son of God who came to save the world. Christianity is one of the three major religions of the world, with about one billion followers. It has a number of branches. The three main divisions are the Roman Catholic, Protestant, and Eastern Orthodox churches.

Jesus, a Jew, laid the foundation for Christianity about 2,000 years ago, when he taught and preached in the area now known as Israel. His beliefs in justice and mercy and the brotherhood of all people attracted a number of followers. But the Roman authorities, fearing a rebellion, had him tried and executed.

For a time after his death, those who accepted the teachings of Jesus continued to practice Judaism. Eventually, though, they became a separate independent group calling themselves Christians.

Christianity grew rapidly in the early days, despite repression by the ruling Romans. By the fourth century A.D., Christianity had become the official religion of the Roman Empire, and Rome had become the center of Christian belief. During the Middle Ages, the Christian Church gained great economic and political power and was the center of learning and culture.

Two major splits, or schisms, have occurred within the Christian Church during its long history. In 1054, it separated into Roman Catholicism, centered in Rome, and the Eastern Orthodox Church, concentrated in Constantinople (now Istanbul), Turkey. The Roman Catholic Church recognizes the pope as its head. The Eastern Orthodox Church rejects the pope's authority.

Then, in the early 1500s, the Church was further divided, as large numbers of Christians broke away in the Protestant Reformation. Among the major Protestant sects that formed were the Baptists, the Lutherans, the Methodists, the Presbyterians, the Puritans, the Quakers, and the Unitarians.

The sacred writings of Christianity include the Hebrew Bible (which is also called the Old Testament) and the New Testament, twenty-seven additional books that were all written before the fourth century. The most important parts of the New Testament are the four Gospels of Matthew, Mark, Luke, and John, which describe the life and teachings of Jesus, and the writings attributed to the apostle Paul. *See also* EASTERN ORTHODOX CHURCH; JESUS; PROTESTANTISM; and ROMAN CATHOLICISM.

CHRISTIAN SCIENCE. A religion based on the use of faith for healing. The Christian Science movement was begun in 1866 by Mary Baker Eddy, who described it as "the scientific system of divine healing." She and fifteen followers founded the Church of Christ, Scientist, in 1879.

The two most important books of Christian Science are the Bible and Eddy's *Science and Health with Key to the Scriptures.* The fundamental message is that only God and His creations are real, and that all He creates is good. Therefore, sickness and sin are not real; they only *appear* real to humans. By fully understanding and accepting this view, Christian Scientists believe it is possible to heal all humans of sickness, sin, grief, failings, and limitations. About 10,000 Christian Science practitioners devote themselves entirely to healing activities. The mother church of Christian Science, the First Church of Christ, Scientist, is located in Boston. *See also* EDDY, MARY BAKER.

CHRISTMAS. A holiday celebrated as the birthday of Jesus. Special religious services are held in church on Christmas Eve, but the day of Christmas is reserved for at-home festivities. Carols are sung telling of Jesus' birth. People exchange gifts in memory of the gifts the Three Wise Men brought to the infant Jesus.

The word *Christmas* has its origin in the old English phrase *Christes Masse,* which means "Christ's Mass." Many symbols are associated with the holiday. The star often put on top of a Christmas tree stems from the reference in the Christian Bible to the star that appeared in the eastern sky signaling the arrival of the Hebrew Messiah, or Savior of the Jews. The Christmas tree itself, an evergreen, may be a symbol for the Tree of Life, representing rebirth and immortality. Santa Claus in America, and Saint Nicholas in some other countries, stands for the gift-giving spirit of Christmas.

The actual date of Christmas is December 25, a day that falls near the winter solstice, the shortest day of the year. Christians probably took this date from pagan winter festivals that occurred around the same time. Jesus' actual birthdate is unknown. Some nationalities, such as the Italians, hold religious cere-monies on Christmas Day but give gifts on the eve of Epiphany, January 6. *See also* EPIPHANY.

CHURCH. A place for Christian worship or any congregation of Christians. Probably the first churches were built late in the third century A.D. Before the Roman Empire became Christian, in 313, Christians worshiped secretly in "house churches." *See also* CATHEDRAL.

CHURCH OF ENGLAND. The official religion of England. The Church of Eng-land is a branch of Christianity that combines both Catholic and Protestant theology.

The Church of England was established during the reign of Henry VIII. The king had quarreled with the pope over the issue of divorce, and, when the pope would not grant him a divorce, Henry declared himself head of the nation-al church in 1534. Under Elizabeth I in 1558, the Church of England became independent of all other Christian movements. Its doctrines are contained in the Book of Common Prayer.

Anglican is a term that applies to the Church of England and those churches that are in communion with it. In the United States, Anglicanism is represented by the Protestant Episcopal Church. *See also* EPISCOPALIANS.

CHURCH OF JESUS CHRIST OF THE LATTER-DAY SAINTS. *See* MOR-MONS.

COLLEGE OF CARDINALS. *See* CARDINAL.

COMMUNION. A Christian ceremony, or sacrament, that repeats in symbolic form the Last Supper. The Last Supper is the name given to the Passover meal celebrated by Jesus and his disciples the night before Jesus' crucifixion. After blessing the bread, Jesus is supposed to have said, "This is my body." And after blessing the wine, he is supposed to have said, "This is my blood." Eating the bread or drinking the wine, therefore, is a way of achieving union with Jesus.

Roman Catholic churches celebrate Communion daily or weekly. The differ-ent Protestant churches observe Communion weekly, monthly, or every three months. Communion is also called Holy Communion or Eucharist. *See also* LAST SUPPER and TRANSUBSTANTIATION.

CONFIRMATION. A ceremony found in both the Christian and Jewish religions that formally admits a person to full membership in the church or synagogue. Roman Catholics, members of the Eastern Orthodox Church, Lutherans, and Anglicans associate confirmation with baptism. In Judaism, boys and girls are confirmed at the age of thirteen. The ceremony for a boy is called a bar mitzvah; for a girl, it is a bas or bat mitzvah. *See also* BAPTISM; BAR MITZVAH; and BAS MITZVAH.

CONFUCIANISM. A traditional Chinese system of ethics, morals, and politics. Confucianism was first taught by the Chinese philosopher, Confucius (551–479 B.C.). The philosophy has had profound influence on traditional Chinese thought, education, and government. About 260 million people in the world today practice Confucianism.

According to Confucianism, the achievement of social harmony and justice depends upon holding the correct attitude toward the five basic relationships: those between ruler and subject; father and son; husband and wife; older and younger brother; and friend and friend. Each relationship has its own particular duties and responsibilities. The ruler must be kindly, the subjects loyal. The father must show love to the son, and the son must honor his father. The husband must treat his wife properly, and in return she must respect him. The older brother must be gracious, the younger humble. Elders must be considerate, juniors respectful. Friends must do to each other as they would have done to them.

The wisdom of Confucius and his disciples appear in the Wu Ching (Five Classics) and the Shih Shu (Four Books). The latter contains the Analects, which are the sayings of Confucius.

Confucianism teaches that the most valuable virtue is that of respect of children for their parents. Chinese culture had depended on a strong family system even before Confucius. Confucius further strengthened Chinese loyalty to the family. The ideal ''superior man'' has self-respect, sincerity, faithfulness, studiousness, a sense of justice, and benevolence, among other virtues. Confucianism has no churches, clergy, or creed. Temples are for carrying out the custom of ancestor worship. *See also* CONFUCIUS.

CONFUCIUS (551–479 B.C.). A great moral philosopher and teacher. Confucius was born in China to a poor but well-respected family, the youngest of eleven children. When he was three years old, his father died, and it is believed that Confucius educated himself. At the age of fifteen, he decided to devote his life to learning. He studied the teachings of the sages (wise men) and became very learned.

After several years he became a teacher and gained a small following of pupils. He wanted to end warfare between states and stop the suffering of the masses at the hands of harsh rulers. He obtained a government post and tried to bring about government reforms.

At fifty years of age, Confucius became minister of justice in the state of Lu. A clash with the authorities, however, soon forced him out of office. For the next thirteen years he wandered from state to state, trying to promote his theories of government. No ruler, though, was willing to put Confucius' ideas into practice. In his old age, Confucius recorded his teachings. His disciples later edited and amplified them in the Five Classics.

Confucius' last years were disappointing and disillusioning. He died at the age of seventy-two, known only to a small band of followers.

Confucius,
551–479 B.C.

After the death of Confucius, the Chinese attempted to stamp out his teachings. But by the first century A.D., attitudes had changed. Shrines were built at which Confucius was honored. By 1068, Confucius was raised to the rank of emperor. In the early twentieth century he was deified. Then, in the 1970s, under Chinese Communist rule, the teachings and worship of Confucius were again suppressed for a time. *See also* CONFUCIANISM.

CONVENT. A religious order isolated from the community. The usual convent is Christian and is for women, who are called nuns or sisters and who have taken vows of chastity, obedience, and poverty.

So-called enclosed convents keep themselves completely apart from the concerns of the outer world. The nuns spend all of their time in prayer, worship, and meditation. Unenclosed convents have different practices. The nuns frequently leave the convent to teach in schools, serve in hospitals, and work in homes for children and the aged, in addition to doing other good works. Many convents are now combining both types of experiences.

The head of a convent is called either a mother superior or an abbess.

CREED. A set of beliefs. Each religion has its own creed, although most creeds have some elements in common. The Nicene Creed, from the Council of Nicaea in A.D. 325, and the Chalcedon Creed, from the Chalcedonian Council of 451, were important in creating the Christian creeds. During the sixteenth century, various Protestant sects adopted their own creeds. The Lutheran creed is the Symbolical Book of the Evangelical Church. The Church of England's creed is the Thirty-nine Articles. And the Presbyterian Church uses Westminster Confessions of Faith.

CRUCIFIXION. The nailing of a person to a cross as a form of execution for a crime. Jesus' death by crucifixion was preceded by various indignities inflicted on him by the Roman authorities. He was mocked, given a crown of thorns, spat on, and beaten. The Gospels report that the Romans nailed Jesus to the cross under the words "Jesus of Nazareth, King of the Jews." After three hours he died and was buried the same day. The crucifixion of Jesus is marked by observances on Good Friday, three days before Easter Sunday. *See also* EASTER; GOOD FRIDAY; and JESUS.

CRUSADES. A series of religious wars undertaken by the Christians of Europe in the eleventh, twelfth, and thirteenth centuries to recapture the Holy Land (Palestine) from the Moslems.

DALAI LAMA. The most important monk within Tibetan Buddhism. The last Dalai Lama was forced to flee Tibet by the Chinese Communists in 1959. Traditionally, the Dalai Lama is selected from among newborn babies upon the death of the last Dalai Lama. The holy men of Tibet consult oracles and look for other magic signs to help them choose the person who will become the Dalai Lama. The person they select is revered by the people, who believe he is a reincarnation of the previous ruler. *See also* LAMAISM.

DAVID. The second king of Israel, who reigned from about 1010 to 970 B.C. David was chosen by the judge Samuel to succeed Saul. He built an empire for his son Solomon and founded a line of rulers. As a boy, armed only with a slingshot, David reputedly killed Goliath, the giant Philistine warrior. Jesus is thought to have descended from David. *See also* SOLOMON.

DAY OF ATONEMENT. *See* YOM KIPPUR.

DEAD SEA SCROLLS. A number of ancient manuscripts found near the Dead Sea, in Israel. The scrolls, written on leather and papyrus, are the oldest existing copies of any parts of the Bible. Included are almost all the books of the Hebrew Bible (the Old Testament), parts of the first Greek translation of the Hebrew Bible (Septuagint), and many other biblical and theological writings.

The first of the Dead Sea Scrolls was found in a cave in the Qumran Valley in 1947 by a Bedouin shepherd boy. In the following years, many other scrolls were found in ten caves in the area. They are from a library belonging to the Essenes, a Jewish sect that lived in the Qumran area from about 200 B.C. to A.D. 68.

The Dead Sea Scrolls can be seen in the Shrine of the Books, a special building that is part of the Israel Museum in Jerusalem. *See also* BIBLE.

DEITY. A person or thing that is revered as a god or goddess.

DEVIL. A figure who in almost all religions symbolizes evil. In primitive religions, devils, or demons, were believed to control the destructive forces of nature. According to the Old Testament, Satan (the Hebrew name for the devil) is the source of sin and the chief obstacle to the will of God. In both Jewish and Christian belief, the devil is a fallen angel who was banished from heaven for rebelling against God, and it is he who leads Adam and Eve to sin. The devil in the Islamic religion is Iblis or Shaltin, who was also originally an angel.

Other names for the devil are Lucifer and Beelzebub. Drawings of the devil from the Middle Ages show him with a tail, horns, and cloven hooves. *See also* ORIGINAL SIN.

The devil, as depicted by H. G. Theaker

DEWALI. A popular Hindu festival that marks the end of the year for Hindus. Dewali usually begins in the middle of November at sundown on the night of the new moon. People use lights to decorate the streets and doorways of their houses. They explode fireworks and honor the gods by holding processions through the streets. Many give parties in their homes and fix traditional holiday dishes.

The new year is also a serious time for Hindus. It is the time to settle all business and religious matters and to forgive all enemies. Many pray to Lakshmi, the goddess of wealth, to ask her blessing for the coming year. *See also* HINDUISM.

DIET OF WORMS. *Diet* means "imperial council"; Worms is a city in Germany. In 1521, Martin Luther appeared before the Holy Roman emperor Charles V at the Diet of Worms to defend his stand on Protestantism. *See also* LUTHER, MARTIN.

Martin Luther, 1483–1546

DURGA PUGA. A ten-day autumn festival that is celebrated by the Hindus. Part of the holiday is given over to reading the *Ramayana*, one of the two epics in the Hindu scriptures. *See also* RAMAYANA.

EASTER. A springtime celebration by which Christians mark the resurrection, or return from death, of Christ, their Savior. The date varies each year, but it always falls on a Sunday between March 22 and April 25 and follows the forty-day period of Lent.

Easter is a day of church attendance, with special religious ceremonies. Every Roman Catholic is required to receive Communion at Eastertime.

Eggs are a special symbol of Easter in many parts of the world. They symbolize the new life that comes to the world in springtime. Bunnies and bonnets and hot cross buns are part of many Easter celebrations. *See also* FEASTS AND FESTIVALS; JESUS; and RESURRECTION.

EASTERN ORTHODOX CHURCH. The Church that split with the pope in Rome in A.D. 1054. Eastern Orthodox churches are the main churches in Greece, the Soviet Union, Eastern Europe, and Western Asia. An estimated 80 million people belong to the Eastern Orthodox religion. The leader is the Ecumenical Patriarch of Constantinople.

Eastern Orthodox churches differ from the Roman Catholic Church mainly in rejecting the authority of the pope. In addition, Eastern Orthodoxy holds to the belief that the Holy Spirit proceeds from the Father. It rejects a phrase later added to the Nicene Creed, called the *filioque*, which states that the Holy Spirit comes from the Son as well as from the Father. Eastern Orthodoxy also disbelieves the idea of the Immaculate Conception.

The three major orders of the Orthodox clergy are bishops, priests, and deacons. Priests may marry, but only before they are ordained. Only unmarried priests can become bishops. Laymen, or nonclergy, may take part in running the church and electing the clergy.

Eastern Orthodox church buildings are usually square. Decorated screens separate the sanctuaries from the main parts of the church. *See also* CHRISTIANITY; IMMACULATE CONCEPTION; and TRINITY.

ECUMENICALISM. A movement, especially among Protestant groups since the 1800s, that aims to achieve unity among Christian denominations. The ecumenical movement works mostly through worldwide interdenominational organizations. These groups cooperate on matters of mutual concern.

**Mary Baker Eddy,
1821–1910**

EDDY, MARY BAKER (1821–1910). Founder of the Christian Science Church. Mary Baker Eddy was born and grew up in New Hampshire. A series of personal misfortunes led her to turn to the Bible for comfort and guidance. She studied the Bible for laws on spiritual healing. Together with her husband, Asa, she established Christian Science in 1877. Two years later, she organized the Church of Christ, Scientist. She began the newspaper, *Christian Science Monitor*, in 1908. *See also* CHRISTIAN SCIENCE.

EED-ES-SAGHEER. A three-day festival that marks the end of the Moslem holy month of Ramadan. Eed-es-Sagheer is a joyous holiday that is celebrated with parties for friends and relatives. *See also* ISLAM.

EIGHT-FOLD PATH. *See* BUDDHISM.

EPIPHANY. A holiday of the Christian Church that is celebrated annually on January 6. Epiphany marks both the birth and baptism of Jesus as well as the meeting of the Three Wise Men with the infant Jesus.

Epiphany is also called Twelfth Day and Little Christmas. In England it marks the end of the Christmas season. Italians present gifts to their children on this day. In the Eastern Orthodox Church it is a time to bless the waters.

EPISCOPALIANS. Members of the Protestant Episcopal Church. The Episcopal Church, which was organized in 1607, was the first American branch of the Church of England. At first, it had few followers. But after the American Revolution, it became independent and began to grow. Today it has about 3 million members in the United States alone.

Episcopalians take the Bible as the word of God. They accept the Trinity and the Virgin Birth. Their prayers and instructions for services are found in the Book of Common Prayer. *See also* CHURCH OF ENGLAND and TRINITY.

EUCHARIST. *See* COMMUNION.

EVANGELISTS. The writers of the four Gospels: Matthew, Mark, Luke, and John. Also, in Protestantism, ministers or other persons who preach at special services. *See also* GOSPELS.

EXCOMMUNICATION. A punishment by which a church bans a member from taking part in its rites and services and thereby denies the person the opportunity to achieve salvation. The Church of England and the Presbyterian Church of Scotland abolished the practice of excommunication by 1700. It is still used by the Roman Catholic Church today.

FAITH. A belief in God or in the doctrines or teachings of religion. Faith is not based on reason or on actual knowledge of God.

FAST. A period of abstaining from all or some food. Almost every religion includes periods of fasting. Generally, the purposes are for penance, to obtain forgiveness for one's sins, or to turn one's thoughts away from the body and toward more spiritual concerns.

Jews fast on Yom Kippur, the Day of Atonement, as repentance for past sins. Moslems fast during the daytime hours of the month of Ramadan. Christians fast during Lent, the period of forty days before Easter.

FEASTS AND FESTIVALS. All religions, from those of the distant past right up to today, have feasts and festivals. Among the oldest that are still observed are the weekly Jewish feasts on Saturday, the Sabbath. Other feasts in the Jewish calendar are connected with spring (Passover) and fall (Rosh Hashanah and Sukkoth). Hanukkah (in December) and Purim (in February or March) came into the Jewish tradition later in history.

The Christian idea of a weekly feast on Sunday derived from the Jewish Sabbath. The principal Christian feasts come in the spring (Easter) and winter (Christmas). Associated with Easter are Ash Wednesday, Good Friday, Palm

Sunday, Pentecost, and Trinity Sunday. Other important observances are All Saints' Day (November 1) and Epiphany (January 6).

People who follow the Moslem religion have two very important festivals. Eed-es-Sagheer is a three-day observance that follows the month of Ramadan. Eed-el-Kebeer lasts about as long, starting on the tenth day of Zu-l-Heggeh, the last month of the Mohammedan year.

Hindus have a spring festival called Holi, which lasts for five days in March or April, and Durga Puga, in October. A holiday very much like Holi, called Hola, is marked by observers of the Sikh religion, which is also practiced in India. The names Hola and Holi come from the word *Holaka*, which is a little like the word *Alleluia* used by Christians.

Among Buddhists, there is a very popular tradition in spring that is called the Flower Festival. It celebrates the birthday of Buddha, the founder of Buddhism. *See also* ALL SAINTS' DAY; CHRISTMAS; DEWALI; DURGA PUGA; EASTER; EED-ES-SAGHEER; EPIPHANY; FLOWER FESTIVAL; GOOD FRIDAY; HANUKKAH; HOLI; HOLY THURSDAY; PALM SUNDAY; PASSOVER; PENTECOST; PURIM; ROSH HASHANAH; and SABBATH.

FIVE PILLARS OF WISDOM. The basic rules of the faith of Islam. They include: (1) belief in Allah as the only God; (2) praying five times a day; (3) helping the poor; (4) keeping the fast of Ramadan; and (5) making a pilgrimage to Mecca. *See also* ISLAM and MECCA.

FLOWER FESTIVAL. An important festival that is celebrated by the Japanese in the spring, to honor the birthday of Buddha. The celebrants decorate the temples with flowers and sprinkle a special scented tea around the holy places of worship. *See also* BUDDHA and BUDDHISM.

FOUR NOBLE TRUTHS. *See* BUDDHISM.

FOX, GEORGE (1624–1691). English religious leader who founded the Society of Friends (the Quakers) around the year 1650. In 1647, George Fox began to preach that every person could receive ''the divine light of Christ'' without the help of trained clergy or special rituals. Over the years he was often attacked by mobs and several times was jailed. His writings were translated widely while he was establishing the Society of Friends, winning him many new recruits. *See also* FRIENDS, SOCIETY OF.

FRANCIS OF ASSISI, SAINT (1182–1226). The founder of an order of the Roman Catholic Church that is devoted to preaching the Gospel and living a life of poverty and service to the poor. The order, known as the Franciscans, received the approval of Pope Innocent III in 1209.

FRIAR. A member of a religious order who originally lived only by begging. Friars differ from monks in several ways. Their basic goal is to bring Christianity to all people. In the past, the order to which a friar belonged could be determined by the color of his robe: Black Friars (Dominicans), Gray Friars (Franciscans), and White Friars (Carmelites).

FRIENDS, SOCIETY OF. A Christian religious group founded around the year 1650 in England by George Fox. The members are called Friends or Quakers. Quakers may have become a nickname because Fox used to warn believers to tremble, or quake, at the word of the Lord. Others say that the name came from members who "quake with emotion" in their religious observance.

Followers of the Friends believe that anyone can achieve communion with Christ. There is no real need for trained clergy or for participating in church rituals. They further believe that there should be no clerical hierarchy.

The Friends are strongly opposed to war, and many refuse to bear arms. They believe in the equality of men and women. Historical foes of slavery, they now work to improve schools, prisons, and mental hospitals. And they refuse to take oaths, since they believe in always speaking the truth anyway. In the past, members of the Society called everyone "thee" and wore plain gray clothes as symbols of equality, but these practices are fading.

The Friends' services are called meetings. The simple buildings in which they gather are meeting houses, not churches. There are no rituals or ceremonies during meetings. Anyone can speak, pray, or preach whenever he or she is moved to do so. In recent years, some Friends have studied at theological schools. There are over 60,000 members of the Society of Friends in the United States today. *See also* FOX, GEORGE.

GNOSTICISM. The beliefs and activities of Gnostics, members of one of the several sects of early Christians. The Gnostics held that only knowledge that came from spiritual insight, not scientific study, could be used to unlock the mysteries of life.

GOD. The divine Supreme Being worshiped by Jews, Christians, and Moslems. Most of the early religions were polytheistic; their worshipers believed in many gods. Most religions today, though, are monotheistic; they believe in only one God. Some people do not believe in the existence of God; these are called atheists. Others say it is impossible to know whether or not there is a God; these are agnostics.

Although Jews believe the name of God cannot be uttered by a human, they use three substitutes in the Hebrew Bible—Adonai, Elohim, and Yahweh. The Christian doctrine believes in the divine Trinity, that God is found in the persons of the Father, the Son, and the Holy Ghost. *See also* TRINITY.

GOLDEN RULE. A rule of conduct that is usually phrased: ''Do unto others as you would have them do unto you.'' According to Matthew 7:12 in the New Testament, Jesus set forth the rule in his Sermon on the Mount. The same precept is found in Judaism and other major religions, as well as in the writings of such philosophers as Confucius.

GOOD FRIDAY. A holy day in the Christian calendar marking the death of Jesus by crucifixion. Good Friday is celebrated with solemn church services on the Friday before Easter Sunday. *See also* CRUCIFIXION; EASTER; and JESUS.

GOSPELS. The first four books of the New Testament. The Gospels were named for the four men, Matthew, Mark, Luke, and John, who are said to have written them. Each book is a collection of the acts and words of Jesus and is meant to be used for teaching.

GRACE. The state of being favored by God. According to Christian belief, one must be in a state of grace to enjoy eternal life. Grace is also a short prayer offering thanks to God before eating a meal.

GRAHAM, BILLY (b. 1918). An American evangelist who preaches before millions of people in all parts of the world. Billy Graham was born in Charlotte, North Carolina, and was ordained a minister in 1940.

HAJJ. In Islam, a pilgrimage to Mecca, the holy city. A person who takes part in a *hajj* is called a *hajji* and is held in great respect for the deed. *See also* ISLAM; MECCA; and PILGRIMAGE.

HANUKKAH. A Jewish holiday, also called the Festival of Lights or the Feast of the Maccabees. The holiday is usually celebrated in December and lasts for

A menorah

eight days. It marks the victory of Judas Maccabee and his brothers over the Syrians in 165 B.C., after a three-year effort by the Syrians to force the Jews to worship Syrian gods. Upon recapturing Jerusalem the Jews cleaned their temple of Syrian idols and rededicated it to God. They found only one jar of oil with which to light their holy lamps. But, miraculously, the cruse burned for eight days. From then on, the festival became an annual observance for Jews.

Each night of Hanukkah, there is a ceremony of lighting the special candles on a candelabra called a menorah. On the first evening one candle is kindled. The following night two are lit. By the last night all eight candles burn on the menorah. During Hanukkah, adults usually give the children a gift on each night of the holiday. It is customary to eat potato pancakes, called *latkes*, as a festive treat. *See also* FEASTS AND FESTIVALS and JUDAISM.

HARE KRISHNA. The sect that follows the teachings of Krishna, who appeared on earth as an incarnation of the Hindu god Vishnu. The story of his appearance is related in the Bhagavad-Gita, a text of Hinduism.

The Hare Krishna movement was brought to New York City in 1965 by His Divine Grace A.C. Bhaktivendanta Swami Prabhupada. Prabhupada interpreted the Hindu beliefs for Western followers, saying Krishna is the same god as the one worshiped by Jews, Christians, and Moslems. He preached that belief in Krishna will bring peace and happiness and that every person has a role in life and need not compete in order to better himself or herself.

People who join the Hare Krishna movement wear Indian dress. The men shave their hair, except for a long tuft at the back. Most live in Hare Krishna temples, where they abstain from the use of drugs, tobacco, and alcohol. The believers spend many hours each day chanting the mantra: "Hare Krishna, Hare Krishna, Krishna Krishna, Hare Hare Hare Rama, Hare Rama, Rama Rama, Hare Hare." This is an aid to meditation. To raise money, followers also spend time begging and selling flowers or other small items. *See also* HINDUISM; MANTRA; and VISHNU.

HASIDISM. A very strict sect of Judaism. Hasidism was founded in Poland in the 1700s by Eliezer Baal Shem-Tov. From there it spread throughout Eastern Europe. Its adherents emphasize mysticism, prayer, religious zeal, and joy in religion. Today most Hasids live in the United States or in Israel.

HEAVEN. In the Judeo-Christian and Islamic beliefs, a place of beauty and peace, where God and the angels are traditionally said to live. Heaven is also the place where the souls of people granted salvation are believed to go after they die, and where they enjoy eternal bliss. Sometimes called Paradise.

HELL. The place to which the souls of sinners and unbelievers are said to be sent after death. The Christian hell is ruled by the devil, and the damned are tormented by the heat of its fires. The Moslem hell is much the same as the Christian inferno. In early Hebrew belief, the dead wandered about in *she'ol*, in an unhappy state of gloom. Judaism later replaced *she'ol* with heaven and hell. In the Hebrew hell, evil souls are sent into everlasting hellfire.

HERESY. An opinion or idea that goes against the accepted beliefs of a church or religious group.

HINDUISM. The chief religion of India. Hinduism dates back to about 2500 B.C. Many consider it the world's oldest organized religion. It has an estimated 475 million followers, most of whom live in India and Nepal.

**Brahman,
the "World Spirit"**

Hindus believe in one supreme and absolute spirit called Brahman, which means "World Soul." They worship three gods whom they consider aspects of the divine Brahman. These gods are Brahma the Creator, Vishnu the Preserver, and Siva the Destroyer. The religion teaches that these three gods evolved from Brahman and are continuously creating and changing the world.

According to Hinduism, every living thing in the world has *atman*, its own soul or spirit. The aim of life is to have one's soul merge, or join, with Brahman. Such unity comes after the soul has been purified in a series of rebirths, or reincarnations. Each good life moves the soul to a higher state. Each evil life leads to rebirth in a lower state. A person who lived an evil life might even be reborn as a plant or an animal. When a soul reaches a state of perfection, it joins the World Soul in a state known as nirvana.

Nirvana can be reached in three ways. One way is through a life of good deeds. Another is the intellectual way, through a life devoted to thought, contemplation, and meditation. And finally, there is faithful devotion to a favorite god. This way is thought to be the easiest path.

Most Hindus try to observe the law of the Action, called *karma*. This law teaches that from good acts must come good results, and from evil acts must come evil results. The consequences of a person's deeds create that person's karma. After someone dies, he or she is reborn to live out the karma, either good or bad.

The rules for caste appear in Hindu scripture. They tell that the Brahman created the first man, Manu. Out of Manu's head came the best and holiest people, the Brahmins, or priests. Out of his arms came the rulers and warriors, the Kshatriyas. Out of his thighs came the Craftsmen, named Vaisyas. And out of his feet came the common people, the Sudras.

Each caste has its own *dharma*, or duties to perform. The priestly Brahmins have religious duties. The ruling class is expected to show self-control and practice nonviolence. The lowest caste, the Sudras, should show proper humility and serve the higher castes. Those who belong to no caste at all, the pariahs, or outcasts, have become known as the "untouchables" in Indian society. Contact with an untouchable, or intermarriage between members of different castes, is a violation of the laws of dharma.

Some Hindus hope to achieve salvation by the strict discipline of mind and body called yoga. By holding specific postures, meditating, and controlling their breathing, those who practice yoga master their physical bodies. Then comes control of the emotions. The various kinds of yoga make possible the total concentration needed to become one with Brahman.

Vishnu the Creator and Siva the Destroyer are the two most important objects of worship in the Hindu religion. Ordinary people, though, usually have a particular god or goddess whom they worship. Nearly every home has its own altar, with statues of personal gods. Most people place small offerings on the altars each day. Religion is very much a part of everyday life. There are separate rituals for almost every activity, from getting up in the morning to preparing for bed at night.

People also worship in the temples and at shrines, where prayer is very individual. The worshiper places a gift, such as flowers or fruit, in front of the god and often gives the priest a small offering, too. Priests take care of the temples but do not conduct services.

Dewali, the Festival of Lights, is a major Hindu holiday.

MH Country School

Religious individuals make pilgrimages to the sacred Ganges River and to shrines all over India. Special temples are devoted to the worship of Hanuman, the monkey god. Monkeys are greatly respected in Hinduism because, according to legend, they helped Rama, one of the incarnations of Vishnu, rescue his wife Sita.

Taking part in festivals is an important part of a Hindu's life. The festival of Holi is a joyous celebration that marks the arrival of spring. One of the biggest festivals is the ten-day-long autumn holiday called Durga Puga, sometimes known as Dasehra. Around the middle of November, Dewali, the Feast of Lights, marks the end of the Hindu year. *See also* BRAHMA; BRAHMAN; DEWALI; DURGA PUGA; HOLI; PILGRIMAGE; SIVA; VISHNU; and YOGA.

HOLI. The Hindu festival that celebrates the coming of spring and honors the god Krishna. The Hindus put on bright clothing and spray one another with colored water and powders. Images of evil spirits are burned in the street. *See also* HINDUISM.

HOLY COMMUNION. *See* COMMUNION.

HOLY GHOST. *See* TRINITY.

HOLY THURSDAY. The Thursday that follows the fifth Sunday (forty days) after Easter. Holy Thursday marks the departure of Christ from earth. Another name for Holy Thursday is Ascension Day.

HYMN. A song in praise of God. The early Christian hymns came from the older Jewish psalms but later developed their own separate style. During the Middle Ages, most Christian hymns were sung in Latin. Two that have survived are "Dies Irae" by Thomas de Celano (who died c. 1260) and "Stabat Mater Dolorosa" by Jacopone da Todi (who died in 1306).

With the Protestant Reformation, hymns were written in the language of their native countries. Martin Luther wrote thirty-seven hymns. The best known of these is "Ein' feste Burg" ("A Mighty Fortress"), composed in 1529.

Among the most famous hymns are: "Abide with Me," 1847; "Faith of Our Fathers," 1864; "Lead, Kindly Light," 1833; "Nearer My God to Thee," 1841; "Onward, Christian Soldiers," 1865; "Rock of Ages," 1775; and "The Battle Hymn of the Republic," 1861.

IDOL. An image, usually of a god or some object of worship. Many societies and religions have their own idols. Jews are forbidden by Hebrew law to make or worship any idol. The religion of Islam also does not allow the making of human or animal figures. Images are used, though not worshiped, in the Christian, Buddhist, and Hindu religions.

IMAM. The leader of a Moslem service in the Islam religion. *See also* ISLAM.

IMMACULATE CONCEPTION. A doctrine of Roman Catholicism. It refers to the fact that the Virgin Mary was born free of Original Sin in order to be pure enough to become the mother of Jesus. *See also* ORIGINAL SIN.

IMMORTALITY. The belief that the soul has eternal life, which continues after the body has died. Almost every religion believes in immortality to some extent. It is a major part of the Christian and Islamic faiths and is also a basic belief of Judaism. Hinduism, Buddhism, and Jainism do not accept immortality as such. They believe in reincarnation, in which the dead are reborn in new bodies or forms. Immortality and the release from the cycle of death and rebirth is attained in Hinduism by achieving freedom from matter and oneness with the

World Soul. In Buddhism, it is achieved through enlightenment, and in Jainism, through freedom from matter.

INQUISITION. An effort by the Roman Catholic Church to seek out and punish persons who disagreed with Church doctrine. The Inquisition was active in many parts of Europe from the Middle Ages on, but it is most often identified with Spain. *See also* SPANISH INQUISITION.

ISAAC. The only son of the Hebrew patriarch Abraham and his wife, Sarah. Because Isaac's parents were very old when he was born, and the people made fun of Sarah for having a child so late in life, Isaac was given a name that means laughter. Ishmael, the ancestor of the Arab peoples, was Isaac's half-brother.

The great test of Abraham's faith came when God ordered him to sacrifice his beloved son Isaac. Abraham agreed but at the last moment was released from the command.

Isaac married Rebekah, who bore him the twins Esau and Jacob. When Isaac was very old and nearly blind, Rebekah tricked him into blessing Jacob instead of Esau, who was the elder and thus by custom entitled to the blessing. Jacob fled but returned twenty years later. According to the Bible, Isaac died at the age of 180 and was buried in the Cave of Machpelah in Israel. *See also* ABRAHAM and ISHMAEL.

ISHMAEL. The elder son of Abraham in the Hebrew Bible. Ishmael's mother was Hagar, a concubine of Abraham's; she and her son were cast out into the wilderness by Abraham's wife, Sarah, who was jealous of her. Ishmael became a mighty warrior and is honored by the Arabs as their ancestor.

ISLAM. The religion based on the teachings of the prophet Mohammed. Islam is the most recent of the three great religions, after Judaism and Christianity, to believe in a single god.

Mohammed was born in the city of Mecca, in what is now Saudi Arabia, around the year 570. In 610 he began to preach a new religion in Mecca. He announced that he had been sent by God as a messenger to let the people know that there is only one God, Allah. He called upon the people to join him in worshiping Allah. Those who accepted Mohammed's teachings were called Moslems, meaning in Arabic ''one who submits.'' The religion is called Islam, an Arabic word that means ''submission.''

**Mohammed,
c. 570–632**

At first Mohammed won few converts. The rich and powerful people of Mecca, in particular, rejected his message. In fact, some were so angered by his teachings and so frightened of what might come of them that they plotted to have him killed.

Mohammed fled from Mecca in 622, going to the city of Yathrib (now Medina). His flight is called the *Hegira*. The Moslem calendar starts from the year of the Hegira. At Medina, his followers gave him refuge and helped him to spread his message. Within a few years, the number of Moslems had grown considerably. In 630, Mohammed and his fellow Moslems returned to Mecca and conquered it.

One target of their attack was the Kaaba, a pagan temple. The Moslems destroyed all the idols that were there and turned the Kaaba into an Islamic place of worship, a mosque. The people of Mecca then accepted Mohammed and the religion of Islam. Mecca and Medina became the sacred cities of the new religion. Mohammed died in A.D. 632.

Mohammed's beliefs and ideas comprised the holy book of Islam, the Koran, or Qur'an. The Koran is considered the word of God as revealed through Mohammed. Parts of the Koran resemble the Old and New Testaments of the Christian Bible. The Koran describes a kind and just God, all-powerful, who created the universe and everything in it, including prophets such as Abraham, Moses, Jesus, and Mohammed to help humans lead purer lives and attain paradise.

To guide individuals in leading moral lives, the Koran defines good and evil acts. It teaches the virtues of faith in God, kindness, honesty, honor, and courage. Moslems must honor their parents, be kind to slaves, protect the weak, and help the poor.

Lying, stealing, and murder are strictly forbidden. The Koran also forbids eating pork, drinking alcohol, gambling, or making human or animal images.

Life for Moslems is a time of testing and preparation for death. At the Last Judgment, a person's guardian angel will bear witness to the record of his or her deeds. Those deeds will then be taken into account in deciding who goes to heaven and who goes to hell. Faith is coupled with deeds in making the final decision. Heaven and hell are much like the states accepted by Christians.

Moslems pray five times a day—at dawn, at noon, in the afternoon, in the evening, and at nightfall. A *muezzin*, or crier, climbs to a *minaret*, or tower, of the mosque and calls the Moslems to worship. The Moslem sabbath is on Friday. Before the traditional noon prayers, the worshipers wash their feet, hands, and faces. Both the leader, or imam, and the devout face Mecca.

There is fasting from dawn to sunset during the month of Ramadan, the ninth month of the Moslem calendar. At the end of the month there is a joyous three-day festival called Eed-es-Sagheer.

Every Moslem is commanded to make at least one *hajj*, or pilgrimage, to Mecca. There the pilgrim walks seven times around the Kaaba and kisses the sacred Black Stone.

By the seventh century, the Moslems had split into two major groups, the Sunnites and the Shiites. Most Moslems, over 560 million, are Sunnites. The Shiites number fewer than 26 million. The Sunnites are found throughout the Middle East, North Africa, and some parts of Pakistan, Indonesia, Turkey, and Albania. The Shiites live mostly in Iraq and Iran. *See also* FIVE PILLARS OF WISDOM; KAABA; KORAN; MECCA; and MOHAMMED.

JACOB. The second son of Isaac and, according to the Hebrew Bible, the father of twelve sons who founded the twelve tribes of Israel.

JAINISM. A religion of India practiced by an estimated 1.5 million people. Jainism arose at the same time as Buddhism, in the sixth century B.C.

A succession of twenty-four Tirthankaras (teachers) are thought to have created the religion. The last, Prince Vardhamana (599–527 B.C.), became known as Mahavira, or the "Great Hero." Upon the death of his parents, the prince decided to renounce his wealth and title and become a beggar-monk. He took the Vow of Silence and meditated on the source of human suffering and the way to find salvation. After twelve years of the strictest discipline, he believed he had the answer to life's problems. He devoted the remaining thirty years of his life to teaching.

At the center of Mahavira's beliefs is *Ahimsa*, a reverence for life and all living things. Jainists believe that everything in the universe has a soul, and all matter is eternal. Therefore, they do not wish to kill or hurt any living thing, even in self-defense. Along with this is a belief in self-denial.

Like the Hindus, Jainists believe in reincarnation. Good deeds during each existence decide whether someone will be reborn in a higher or lower state. After a number of incarnations, a person may attain nirvana. But unlike Hinduism, Jainism does not consider nirvana to be a union with Brahman. To Jainists, there is no supreme World Spirit.

The Jain temples are among the most beautiful in India. Each one contains an image of the twenty-four teachers of Jainism. Worshipers pray to them and make offerings, usually of rice. Followers belong to one of two sects: the Shvetambara, whose priests wear only white, and the Digambara, whose priests wear only loin cloths.

JEHOVAH. The ancient Hebrew word used to refer to God. Other words include Yahweh, Elohim, and Adonai. Jews use these terms because it is forbidden by Jewish law to use the true name of the Supreme Being. *See also* GOD.

JEHOVAH'S WITNESSES. A religious group organized in Pennsylvania during the 1870s by Charles Taze Russell (1852–1916). The Witnesses believe in the second coming of Christ and take most of their ideas from writings in the New Testament Book of Revelation.

According to Jehovah's Witnesses, when Christ returns there will be a great battle at Armageddon between him and the forces of evil. The wicked will be defeated, and for the following thousand years Christ will reign on earth.

At the end of this time, the devil will appear for a brief while. Then he and his followers will be destroyed, and heaven will be established on earth.

Jehovah's Witnesses have no churches but worship in Kingdom halls. There are no special ministers. Each member is considered to be a minister of the gospel.

As part of their religious views, Jehovah's Witnesses do not approve of the use of liquor or tobacco and do not recognize divorce. They also do not accept the notion of saluting the flag, claiming it is similar to worshiping an idol.

The Witnesses spread their message by way of a very active publishing program of magazines, books, and pamphlets. The magazine *Watchtower* is their main publication.

Today there are over 500,000 Jehovah's Witnesses worldwide. The main headquarters are located in Brooklyn, New York.

JESUITS. Members of a Roman Catholic religious order called the Society of Jesus, founded by Saint Ignatius Loyola in 1534 and devoted to missionary and educational work. Jesuits take vows of poverty, chastity, and obedience.

JESUS. The central figure of the Christian religion. Most of the information about the life of Jesus comes from the Gospels of Matthew, Mark, Luke, and John as found in the New Testament of the Christian Bible. The name *Jesus* is the Greek translation of the Hebrew name *Joshua*, which means "Jehovah is salvation." *Christ* was a title given to Jesus after his death. It means "anointed one" and refers to the coming of the Messiah, or Savior, the Jews had prophesied. Although Jesus was a Jew, he was not accepted by Jews as the Messiah whom God had promised would come.

No one is sure of the year or day of Jesus' birth. It is known, however, that it was sometime during the reign of Herod, who died in the year 4 B.C. Therefore, the modern calendar that started A.D. 1 (A.D. stands for *Anno Domini*, or "year of our Lord") is probably wrong. And the practice of celebrating Jesus' birth on December 25 seems to have no basis in fact. This day was probably selected because the pagan sun god was worshiped around this time in December.

Little is known of the childhood of Jesus. When he was thirty, though, it is believed that he started to preach. He was baptized by John the Baptist. As he sermonized about the Kingdom of God, a number of followers joined him and helped to spread his word.

The Gospels contain descriptions of thirty-six miracles that Jesus performed. He is said to have turned water into wine, divided five loaves of bread and two fish among 5,000 people so that everyone had enough to eat, walked on water, healed the sick, and brought the dead back to life.

Near the end of his life, the Jewish authorities and Roman officials became very fearful of Jesus. At the Last Supper, he announced that one of the twelve disciples present would betray him. Later that night, while Jesus was praying on the Mount of Olives, he was pointed out by Judas Iscariot and was arrested.

On the following day, a Friday, Jesus was crucified by the Romans and buried. The Gospels report that when his followers went to the tomb on Sunday, it was empty. The Christian religion holds that Jesus was resurrected and that over the next forty days he appeared to the eleven faithful disciples, taught them, and commanded them to preach God's word to all. Then he rose up to heaven. *See also* CHRISTIANITY; CRUCIFIXION; EASTER SUNDAY; GOOD FRIDAY; LAST SUPPER; RESURRECTION and ROMAN CATHOLICISM.

JOHN, SAINT. Saint John the Evangelist was considered the most loyal of Jesus' twelve apostles. The fourth Gospel in the New Testament is generally credited to Saint John. *See also* GOSPELS.

JOHN THE BAPTIST (c. 7 B.C.–A.D. 28). The great prophet who predicted the coming of Jesus. John the Baptist received his name because he baptized people in the waters of the River Jordan. The New Testament tells how Jesus, his cousin, came to him to be baptized.

JOSEPH. The eleventh of the twelve sons of Jacob. The story of how Joseph was sold into slavery by his brothers and became a great ruler in Egypt is told in the Book of Genesis in the Hebrew Bible. Joseph was also the name of the husband of Mary, Jesus' mother.

JUDAISM. The religion of the Jewish people. Judaism originated at a time and in a part of the world where most people believed in the existence of many gods; this was known as polytheism. Judaism taught that there is only one God, a belief called monotheism.

The basis of Judaism is trust in a just God. Followers believe in an afterlife. But they are more concerned with living a moral and ethical life here on earth than in preparing for the next world.

The first outstanding figure in Judaism was Abraham, who is said to have lived about 1800 B.C. Jews believe that God made a covenant, or agreement, with Abraham in which Abraham promised God that he would carry the message of one God to the world.

Tradition holds that the Jewish people were led out of slavery in Egypt by Moses in the thirteenth century B.C. Moses is credited with receiving the Ten Commandments, the Jewish code of ethics, from God and giving them to his people to live by.

Some time after the Israelites settled the Promised Land of Canaan (now part of Israel), King Solomon built a temple in Jerusalem. This temple was destroyed by the Babylonians in 586 B.C. A second temple was built; it was later annihilated by the Roman army in A.D. 70. After Rome defeated the last of the Jewish resisters in A.D. 135, the Jews were expelled from Jerusalem, their capital and center of worship.

The Jewish people became scattered throughout the Middle East and Europe. Wherever they settled, they built synagogues as houses of worship and centers of Jewish life. Rabbis became the religious leaders and teachers of the people.

From that time on, Jews prayed that one day they would return to their homeland. Zionism began as a movement that sought to return Jews to their own state. In 1948, after the Nazi Holocaust took the lives of 6 million Jews during World War II, the State of Israel was established.

The most sacred text of Judaism is the Torah, or Pentateuch, which is the first five books of the Hebrew Bible. The Torah sets out the Jewish law. The Talmud, completed in the fifth century A.D., is a separate collection of laws that includes the Mishnah, or oral law, in Hebrew, and the Gemara, a commentary in Aramaic. The two interpret the meaning of the original scriptures.

Judaism has three major branches or denominations: Orthodox, Reform, and Conservative. The Orthodox branch stresses strict observance of the Torah. Orthodox Jews pray three times a day. The men keep their heads covered at all times with skullcaps, called yarmulkes, as a sign of respect to God. In Orthodox services the men and women sit separately. Prayers are mostly in Hebrew.

The Reform movement began in the early 1800s. Many Reform Jews do not recognize the Talmud as authoritative and do not strictly observe its teachings. Reform Jews stress the importance of secular (worldly) values. They believe that the principles of Judaism are more important than the practices. Some have given up most of the ritual observances. Services are mostly in the language of the country in which they are held.

Conservative Jews are like the Orthodox in that they keep to the traditional practices of Judaism. They are like the Reform Jews in their desire to adapt to modern living. Although they accept the Torah, they are willing to fit it to modern times. In the early 1900s, a group broke away from the Conservatives. They call themselves Reconstructionists. Originated by Mordecai M. Kaplan, they consider Judaism an evolving religious civilization. Altogether, there are 15 million Jews in the world.

Services in the synagogue consist of prayer, a talk by the rabbi, and a reading of the Torah. The Torah used in the synagogue is written on special scrolls that are kept in the ark, or sacred chest.

Sabbath is observed from sunset Friday to sunset Saturday. It is a time of prayer, rest, and readings.

Major festivals include Passover, Rosh Hashanah, Yom Kippur, Hanukkah, and Sukkoth. *See also* ABRAHAM; BIBLE; FEASTS AND FESTIVALS; MOSES; TALMUD; and TEN COMMANDMENTS.

JUDAS ISCARIOT. One of the twelve disciples of Jesus. Judas betrayed Jesus with a kiss. He revealed him to his enemies for thirty pieces of silver.

K

KAABA. The most holy shrine of Islam. Found in Mecca, the Kaaba is a small building in the shape of a cube. The sacred Black Stone is in the south wall.

Mohammed replaces the Black Stone in the Kaaba after conquering the city of Mecca.

Moslems from all over are urged to make at least one pilgrimage, or *hajj*, to the Kaaba. They walk around the building seven times and then kiss the Black Stone. According to Islamic belief, the Kaaba was built by Abraham and his son Ishmael. Abraham, it is said, was given the Black Stone by the angel Gabriel. *See also* ISLAM.

KARMA. *See* HINDUISM.

KNOX, JOHN (1505–1572). A religious reformer and historian who led the Protestant Reformation in Scotland. *See also* REFORMATION.

KORAN. The sacred book of Islam. The Moslems believe that the Koran contains the Word of God as revealed to Mohammed over the prophet's lifetime. The text was probably first transcribed by Zaid ibn-Thabit, secretary to Mohammed. In A.D. 651, the caliph Othman established ibn-Thabit's writings as the holy book of the Islamic faith.

The Koran is divided into 114 chapters, or *suras*. Each varies in length from a few lines to hundreds of verses.

All Moslems turn to the Koran for help in practicing their religion and for guidance in living a moral life. Many Moslems learn sections of the Koran by memory. *See also* CALIPH and ISLAM.

KOSHER. A word from the Hebrew that means "fit to be eaten." According to the strict laws of the Jewish religion, certain foods may not be eaten and others have restrictions attached to them.

The rules of the Talmud prescribe that Jews may not eat pork or shellfish. Meat must be bought from kosher butchers, who slaughter the animals in a specific way, quickly and without pain to the animal. All blood must be removed from the meat by washing, soaking, and salting.

Meat must not be eaten with milk or dairy products. Dishes and utensils for meat may not be used for dairy foods. Three hours must elapse after meat has been eaten before milk can be drunk.

KRISHNA. A human incarnation of the god Vishnu the Preserver. Krishna is one of the most important and popular Indian deities. He appears in the Bhagavad-Gita, an important Hindu text. *See also* HINDUISM and VISHNU.

L

LAMAISM. A form of Buddhism that is practiced in Tibet, Mongolia, and parts of China. Lamaism is a form of the Mahayana Buddhism of India, from which it sprang during the seventh century A.D. The name comes from the Tibetan word *lama*, the title of monks of a higher rank. The leading lama, the Dalai Lama, was both the spiritual and political leader of the Tibetan people. The present Dalai Lama lives in exile in India with Tibetan refugees. *See also* BUDDHISM and DALAI LAMA.

LAO-TZU. The founder of Taoism. Lao-tzu is believed to have been born in 604 B.C. in the Honan province of China. The date of his birth is disputed. Some scholars even suggest that Lao-tzu was a fictional character invented by Taoists to establish a historical connection with Confucius.

The name means "the old philosopher" in Chinese. According to legend, Lao-tzu was born after sixty years of gestation, as an old man with white locks. Originally he was called Li Erh. He lived the life of a recluse and became a librarian in the Chou court. He is said to have met Confucius in 517 B.C. and criticized the younger man for studying the ancients and for being proud and ambitious.

In his old age, Lao-tzu became troubled by his superiors. He decided to leave his government post and travel west. It is said that the gatekeeper persuaded him to write down his philosophy before he crossed the border.

**Lao-tzu,
seventh century** B.C.

Legend has it that Lao created the *Tao Te Ching* (*The Way and the Power*), a treatise that became the basis of Taoist philosophy and religion. Scholars say, however, that the text dates from the middle of the third century, several centuries after Lao-tzu was supposed to have lived. *See also* TAOISM.

LAST SUPPER. The meal that Jesus and his twelve disciples are said to have eaten before Jesus was crucified.

Toward the end of his life, Jesus knew he had many enemies in Jerusalem but felt it was his duty to go there and preach. He arrived in Jerusalem during the week of Passover and was very well received by the people. The Gospels report that the Jewish priests, though, became angry when Jesus went to the temple and drove out the money lenders.

Jesus spent the next few days teaching and praying. On Thursday night he is said to have attended a seder, or Passover meal, with his twelve disciples. (The Gospel of Saint John reports that the Last Supper took place on a Wednesday and was an ordinary meal.)

At this time he announced that one of his disciples would betray him. As Jesus served the bread at this meal, he said, "This is my body." And as he served the wine, he said, "This is my blood." This later became the basis for the Communion service. Later that night, Jesus was taken prisoner by the Roman soldiers and on the following day was crucified.

The Last Supper is a favorite subject of artists. The most famous depiction is the painting by Leonardo da Vinci. It can be found on a wall of the monastery of Santa Maria della Grazie in Milan, Italy. *See also* COMMUNION and CRUCIFIXION.

Belgian artist Dierik Bouts painted this depiction of the Last Supper.

LATTER-DAY SAINTS. *See* MORMONS.

LAZARUS. A brother of Mary and Martha whom Jesus loved. Lazarus became ill and died. Jesus is said to have come to Lazarus' tomb four days later and raised him from the dead.

LENT. The forty-day period before Easter, a time of religious observance by Christians. Lent is significant in several ways. It is a reminder of Jesus' forty-day fast in the wilderness, as well as a time to prepare spiritually for Easter. It is also an official period of mourning for the death of Jesus.

The name *Lent* is from the old English word *lencten*, which means "spring."

Lent begins on Ash Wednesday and ends on Easter Sunday. The day before Lent, called Shrove Tuesday, is a feast time. Shrove Tuesday is also often called Mardi Gras, which is French for "Fat Tuesday." For up to a week before Lent, there are carnivals, parades, balls, and dancing in the street.

During the forty days of Lent there are special church services. These observances reach a climax on Easter Sunday. Many Christians fast, do penance, contribute to charities, and renounce various pleasures during Lent. The last week of Lent is called Holy Week. *See also* EASTER.

LITURGY. A form of public worship in Christian churches. Often, liturgy refers to the celebration of the Eucharist, or Holy Communion. *See also* COMMUNION.

LORD'S PRAYER. The prayer given by Jesus to his disciples. One version of it reads: "Our Father who art in heaven,/Hallowed be thy name./Thy Kingdom come./Thy will be done,/As in heaven so on earth./Give us this day our daily bread/And forgive us our debts/As we have forgiven our debtors./And bring us not into temptation./Deliver us from the evil one." The Lord's Prayer can be found in the Gospels of Matthew and Luke in the Christian Bible.

LUKE, SAINT. An early disciple of Christ and a close companion of Paul. Luke is widely thought to be the author of the third Gospel in the Christian New Testament. *See also* GOSPELS.

LUTHER, MARTIN (1483–1546). German-born leader of the Protestant Reformation. Luther was ordained a priest of the Roman Catholic Church in 1507. He taught at a university and preached in the Castle Church in Wittenberg.

Luther was greatly troubled by the Catholic Church's sale of indulgences. The selling of indulgences allowed people to buy forgiveness for their sins.

In 1517, Luther made public his objections to indulgences and other Church abuses by nailing a list of these abuses on the door of the Castle Church. By this protest, which became known as the Ninety-five Theses, Luther hoped to encourage debate within the Church. He did not intend to quarrel with the pope or revolt against the Church. Nevertheless, the Ninety-five Theses created a storm of reaction and marked the beginning of the Protestant Reformation.

Luther departed from Roman Catholicism even further when, in 1519, he publicly denied the supreme power of the pope. In response, the pope excommunicated him—banned him from the Church. This caused Luther to burn the papal bull (decree) of excommunication. The pope then ordered Luther to appear before the Diet of Worms, a gathering of German priests and nobles. This group demanded that Luther retract his statements. When he refused, he was declared a heretic, a nonbeliever.

On the way home from the city of Worms, a band of masked men seized Luther. They took him to the Castle of Wartburg for his own safety. During the eight months he was there, Luther began to translate the New Testament from the original Greek into German. His work during this period led to the organization of a new church.

Luther returned to Wittenberg in March 1522. In the years following there were many disagreements among the reformers on what the exact beliefs of the new church should be. Luther was unbending in his views. Some of his followers left to organize churches that were closer to their own ideas.

Luther did not insist on new forms of worship for his church. He was mainly concerned with the individual's faith in God, which he believed was the only way to achieve salvation. But many changes did occur. Services were held in the language spoken by the people instead of Latin, which continued to be used in the Roman Catholic mass. Also, the congregation played a more important role in the services, including the singing of hymns.

Luther continued to teach, preach, and write until the end of his life. He was buried in the church at Wittenberg where he had nailed his Ninety-five Theses. *See also* DIET OF WORMS; PROTESTANTISM; and REFORMATION.

LUTHERANS. Members of the Lutheran Church, the oldest denomination of the Protestant faith. Lutherans believe in the principles of Martin Luther, one of the leaders of the Protestant Reformation.

A basic belief of Lutherans is that the guide to salvation is found in the Christian Bible. Lutherans hold that an individual can reach God through his or her faith alone. Lutherans say also that the church's rites and rituals have meaning only as aids to faith. The Lutheran doctrine was set out in the Augsburg Confession, which was written by Luther and others in 1530.

The Lutheran Church is the largest of the Protestant churches. There are over 100 million Lutherans. About one out of every three Protestants worldwide is a Lutheran. More than 8 million Lutherans live in the United States; about 40 million live in Germany. Lutheranism is the official religion of Denmark, Iceland, Norway, Sweden, and Finland—countries where there are some 25 million members. *See also* LUTHER, MARTIN; PROTESTANTISM; and REFORMATION.

MAGI (sing. MAGUS). Priests from ancient Persia. The magi were believed to have supernatural powers, and their name gave rise to the word *magic*. The Three Wise Men who brought gifts to the infant Jesus, named Melchior, Balthasar, and Gaspar, were believed to be magi. Zoroaster is thought to have been a magus also. *See also* ZOROASTER.

MANTRA. Sacred words to be recited or sung. Mantras are used in Hinduism as aids to meditation. *See also* HINDUISM.

MARK, SAINT. One of the four Evangelists. Mark is traditionally believed to be the author of the second Gospel in the Christian New Testament. *See also* GOSPELS.

MARRIAGE. The ceremony that joins a man and a woman as husband and wife. Each religion has its own way of celebrating the marriage ceremony.

Roman Catholics are married at a nuptial mass. The couple kneels at the altar. The priest says special prayers and blessings and sprinkles the couple with holy water.

Protestants are usually wed in a special ceremony that is not part of a regular service. It includes prayers and a sermon by the minister. The bride and groom then exchange vows.

The Jewish marriage ceremony takes place under a canopy. The rabbi offers the prayers and drinks some wine, with both the bride and groom later sipping from the same cup. Sometimes, the groom and bride take turns walking around each other. At the end of the ceremony, the groom smashes a wine glass with his foot. This is a reminder of the destruction of Solomon's Temple in Jerusalem, a sad note injected at this time of great happiness.

Above: a Jewish marriage ceremony. *Right:* a Greek Orthodox wedding service.

Quakers are married in a very simple ceremony. The couple go before a special meeting and declare their desire to marry. Acting as witnesses, everyone signs the marriage certificate, and the ceremony is completed.

The central part of the Hindu marriage ceremony is the seven steps taken together by the bride and groom around the sacred fire. A Japanese Shinto couple seals their marriage by drinking a cup of wine in front of a priest.

MARY. *See* VIRGIN MARY.

MASS. The Communion service of the Roman Catholic Church. Mass is also used to refer to the Episcopalian service.

The priest who performs the mass is called the celebrant. The ceremony takes place at an altar. For High Mass, there is music and singing, and the celebrant is assisted by a deacon and subdeacon, both of whom are usually priests. The more common Low Mass requires only one priest, and there is neither music nor incense.

Most of the mass remains the same from celebration to celebration. These unchanging parts are called the "ordinary." Other sections, the "proper," change with the day or the occasion. Among the proper masses are the nuptial mass for weddings and the requiem mass for funerals.

MATTHEW, SAINT. One of the four Evangelists who was also one of Jesus' twelve apostles. Saint Matthew is considered the author of the first Gospel. *See also* GOSPELS.

MECCA. The holy city of Islam, located in Saudi Arabia. Mecca is the birthplace of Mohammed, the founder of Islam. The central shrine for all Moslems is the Kaaba, a small, cube-shaped building located in an open courtyard in Mecca. No matter where they are, Moslems throughout the world face Mecca when they pray. According to Islam, it is the duty of every Moslem to make at least one pilgrimage, or *hajj*, to Mecca. *See also* ISLAM.

MENNONITES. A sect of Protestantism. The name comes from Menno Simons, a Dutch religious reformer. Using the Christian Bible as the source of all their beliefs, the Mennonites baptize adult believers but not infants. Mennonites are nonviolent and refuse to take oaths. They are not much concerned with worldly matters. In the past they have dressed and lived simply and have generally worked as farmers.

Mennonites were once persecuted in many parts of the world. In 1683, William Penn offered them freedom to come to the colony of Pennsylvania, and many settled there. A number of groups have developed within the Mennonite Church. The Amish, for example, separated from the Mennonites in the late seventeenth century. *See also* MENNO SIMONS.

MENNO SIMONS (1496–1561). A Dutch religious reformer. The name of the Mennonite sect derives from his name. Menno Simons was originally a Roman Catholic priest. In 1536, he found that he no longer believed in infant baptism and some other Church teachings. He became an active organizer of a reform movement in Holland and Germany that became a sect of Protestantism. *See also* MENNONITES and PROTESTANTISM.

MESSIAH. The word means the "anointed one" in Hebrew. According to the prophets of the Hebrew Bible, the Messiah would be a person sent by God to restore Israel and bring peace and justice to all. He would be a high priest, a descendant of King David. Jews still await the arrival of such a leader.

Christians believe that Jesus was the Messiah. In fact, the name *Christ* means "Messiah" in Greek. Christians also believe that Jesus will come again as Christ to rule on earth. This belief in the "Second Coming" of Christ is similar to the Jewish belief that the Messiah will return to earth to rule with God.

METHODISTS. One of the denominations of the Protestant Church. Methodism was founded in England by John Wesley in the mid-1700s. The name comes from John Wesley's belief that salvation should be guided by method.

Wesley was an ordained minister of the Church of England and regarded his Methodist "societies" as part of that church. He had no desire to break with it. But in time, he found himself in dispute with the Church of England over doctrine. Wesleyan Methodists separated from the Church of England by degrees and only finally separated altogether after Wesley's death.

At first the new church was called the United Societies. Later it became the Methodist Church. Since then there have been any number of splits, unions, and changes in organization. But Methodism remains a major branch of Protestantism, with 10 million members in the United States today and many other Methodists around the world. *See also* CHURCH OF ENGLAND; PROTESTANTISM; SALVATION; and WESLEY, JOHN.

MINISTER. A member of the clergy in any one of the Protestant churches. The minister conducts services, preaches, and looks after the spiritual life of the members of the congregation. Another name for minister is pastor.

MISSIONARIES. People who work to spread religion and to convert others to their faith. Although a few other religions, such as Buddhism and Islam, have missionaries, the Christian religion has been especially active in its missionary efforts.

The twelve apostles, or disciples, of Jesus were told by Jesus to go forth and preach his gospel. These were the first Christian missionaries. Over the following centuries many other Christian missionaries traveled throughout Europe and parts of Asia, spreading the word of Jesus. In the fifteenth and sixteenth centuries, missionaries often went along on the voyages of exploration, to North and South America, the Orient, and India.

In the seventeenth century, some of the Protestant sects began sending out missionaries. At first they stayed in their own countries. But in time they became active throughout the world.

Missionaries try to establish churches wherever they go. They also build schools and hospitals. Many of the missionaries who came to America erected mission buildings. Some of these still exist in California and the Southwest.

MOHAMMED (c. 570–632). Founder of the religion of Islam and known as the Prophet.

Mohammed was born in Mecca, now part of Saudi Arabia, and traveled widely as a young man. At the age of twenty-five he married an elderly widow and opened a shop in Mecca. He became known as a wise and reverent man.

Sometime later, it is said, Mohammed was praying alone in a cave on Mount Hira when God sent the angel Gabriel to him. The angel announced that Mohammed was to be a prophet and spread the word that there was only one God, but that only Mohammed's closest relatives were to know at first. Because the Arabs at that time were polytheistic, Mohammed's teachings were considered revolutionary.

It was not until A.D. 616 that Mohammed actually began to preach in public. Some of the leaders of Mecca were angered by his teachings. In time, Mohammed had to flee Mecca. He went to the city of Yathrib, now known as Medina, in honor of Mohammed. (*Medina* means ''City of the Prophet.'') His flight, called the *Hegira*, on July 16, 622, marks the start of the Moslem calendar.

By this time, however, the number of Mohammed's followers, as well as his power, had grown considerably. Mohammed became both the religious and political leader of Yathrib and put a number of his ideas into effect. For example, he ended the practice of avenging one murder with another, the killing of unwanted newborn girls, the marriage of one man to many wives, and the worship of idols. He also made laws to protect slaves and the poor.

Several times, warriors from Mecca tried unsuccessfully to conquer Mohammed and his followers. Finally, in 630, Mohammed led an attack on Mecca. He quickly conquered the city and was widely accepted by the people. He destroyed the pagan idols in the Kaaba and made it the holiest shrine of the new religion of Islam. Two years later Mohammed died and was buried in the Prophet's Mosque in Medina. *See also* ISLAM; KAABA; and KORAN.

MONASTERY. A communal home and place of worship for people who choose to devote their lives to religious purposes. Typically, monasteries are all male. The men are called monks or brothers.

The monastic way of life is an important practice in a number of religions. In Buddhism and Hinduism, monastic groups have existed since ancient times. A pre-Christian Jewish sect, the Essenes, was monastic.

Monasteries were organized early in the history of the Christian religion. Groups of men took religious vows in which they promised to devote all their energies to serving God. Monks also vowed never to marry. They worshiped, meditated, and performed good works. In some orders, they did not speak, eat meat, or drink alcohol.

Some monasteries are enclosed. This means the monks spend all their time within the monastery and have almost no contact with the outside world. At unenclosed monasteries, monks go out either for religious or charitable work or to raise the funds necessary to support the monastery. The leader of a monastery is usually called an abbot and holds the position for life.

MONK. *See* MONASTERY.

MONOTHEISM. The belief in one God. The three great monotheistic religions are Judaism, Christianity, and Islam.

MORMONS. The popular name for members of the Church of Jesus Christ of Latter-Day Saints. Their name comes from the title of the sacred book, the Book of Mormon.

Mormons believe that church doctrine comes from the Christian Bible, the Book of Mormon, and other holy writings.

There are no professional Mormon clergy. Any male member can lead a service. Followers do not use tobacco, alcohol, tea, or coffee. Only one person at a time, the president of the church, may receive revelations from God.

The history of the religion dates back to 1820, when Joseph Smith, then a teenager living in New York State, claimed that God appeared to him. Three years later, the angel Moroni is said to have come to Smith and to have told him of a message written upon gold plates that were hidden near Palmyra, New York. Smith is said to have found the plates in 1827 and translated the writings, which were published as the Book of Mormon. The Book tells of ancient prophets who had lived in America from 600 B.C. to A.D. 420, having come from an Israelite colony. In the years following the publication of the Book of Mormon, Smith claimed that several heavenly messengers told him to establish a new church based on the Bible and the Book of Mormon. On April 6, 1830, Smith and his followers organized this church in Fayette, New York.

During the 1830s, the Mormons moved west, establishing communities in Ohio and Missouri. But their neighbors resented them, and they were forced to move and seek new places to settle. In 1840 they founded the city of Nauvoo in Illinois, which soon became the largest city in the state.

In 1844, Smith declared his candidacy for president of the United States. At the same time, a revolt took place among some of the church members. Smith was accused of treason for the methods he used to suppress his enemies, and he was jailed. Not long after, on June 27, 1844, a mob attacked the jail in which he was being held and killed him.

The leadership of the church passed to the governing body, called the Council of the Twelve Apostles. Their senior member, Brigham Young, became president. Mob violence against the Mormons increased, due to certain unpopular Mormon practices. So Young led them west, to the Great Salt Lake. They applied for admission to the United States as the state of Deseret. Statehood was not granted, but Brigham Young was appointed governor of the newly formed Territory of Utah.

Conflicts between the Mormons and their non-Mormon neighbors continued. One point of disagreement was over the Mormon practice of polygamy, one man marrying two or more wives. The church finally ended the practice in 1890, under pressure from the U.S. government.

Today's 3 million Mormons are chiefly clustered around the main temple in Salt Lake City or the twelve other Mormon temples around the world. Only Mormons are allowed into these buildings. Many meeting houses also serve for education and recreation. The Mormon Tabernacle in Salt Lake City has a choir that is world-famous.

MOSES. The legendary lawgiver and prophet of Judaism. Tradition attributes to Moses the development of a system of law and morality that still applies to daily life today. According to some scholars, the Pentateuch, or Five Books of Moses, were actually written by later Jewish lawmakers.

The Hebrew Bible tells that Moses was born in Egypt to Israelite parents. When the pharaoh ordered that all newborn Israelite children be killed, Moses' mother hid him in a basket on the bank of the Nile River. One of the pharaoh's daughters found the baby, took him to the palace, and raised him as her adopted son. Moses' mother became his nurse and taught him about his people.

As a young man, Moses is said to have seen an Egyptian beating an Israel-ite. He killed the Egyptian and, to save his life, had to flee the country. He took refuge with a priest named Jethro and married Jethro's daughter, Zipporah.

One day, Moses was called by God to return to Egypt and free his people from slavery there. God told Moses to lead the Israelites into the Promised Land, Palestine, in the land of Canaan. Moses did as he was commanded, but the pharaoh and his army pursued them. At the edge of the Red Sea, God told Moses to stretch forth his rod. The waters are then said to have parted, and the Israelites were able to walk across. As soon as the Israelites were safely across, the waters flowed back in. The pharaoh and his army were drowned.

Moses led his people to Mount Sinai. Here, the Hebrew Bible says, he received the Ten Commandments from God. God also told Moses how to set up a tabernacle, or sanctuary, for worship. Moses gave the Israelites a code of laws and a legal system to help them govern themselves in the Promised Land.

Because they had worshiped idols or doubted God's word, neither Moses nor any of the older generation was allowed to enter the Promised Land. The Jews are said to have wandered in the wilderness for forty years. Before Moses died, however, he was allowed a glimpse of the Promised Land. *See also* PASSOVER.

MOSLEM. A member of the Islamic religion; a follower of Mohammed. *See also* ISLAM.

MOSQUE. A house of worship in the Islamic religion. All mosques have certain features in common. The *maksoura*, or prayer hall, is a roofed rectangle that opens to a court on one long side. In the middle of the long wall is the *mihrab*, or prayer niche, which faces the direction of Mecca. To its right is the *minbar*, or pulpit.

Mosques also have an open court with a fountain, where worshipers wash their faces, hands, and feet before prayers. In addition, there are one or more *minarets*, or towers, from which the people are called to prayer. *See also* ISLAM.

A mosque

MUSLIM. Another spelling for Moslem. *See also* ISLAM and MOSLEM.

MYTH. A traditional story, usually involving gods or goddesses, invented by people to explain the world and events they do not understand. Myths have an instructional as well as religious purpose. They inform people what they must do to please the gods. A mythology is a collection of myths from a particular culture or group.

NEW TESTAMENT. Part of the Christian Bible, consisting of twenty-seven separate books, which was added to the Hebrew Bible by the early Christians. Christians refer to the Hebrew Bible as the Old Testament. *See also* BIBLE.

NOAH. The Hebrew patriarch who is said to have built a vessel, called the Ark, in which he, his family, and animals of every species were able to survive the

Noah's Ark, depicted in a print by Currier & Ives

flood God sent to cleanse the earth of corruption. The story of Noah and the Flood is related in Genesis, the first book of the Hebrew Bible.

NOVENA. A series of prayers in the Roman Catholic Church. The devotion takes place during the nine days before a religious feast. Novenas are also made to saints to ask their help in specific matters. The practice comes from the nine days of apostolic prayer that lasts from Ascension Thursday to Pentecost. *See also* APOSTLES; HOLY THURSDAY; PENTECOST; and ROMAN CATHOLICISM.

OLD TESTAMENT. The first part of the Christian Bible, consisting of thirty-nine separate books. This portion of the Christian Bible is the same as the Hebrew Bible. *See also* BIBLE.

ORIGINAL SIN. The tendency in all humans toward evil that Christians say descended from Adam and Eve's disobedience in the Garden of Eden.

"The Expulsion from the Garden of Eden," by artist J. Schnorr von Carolsfeld

According to the Bible, Adam was the first human. Eve was created from Adam's rib to be his helpmate. Eve was tempted by a serpent to eat fruit from the Tree of Knowledge of Good and Evil, although God had expressly forbidden it. Eve then convinced Adam to do likewise. As a result, they were both cast out from the Garden of Eden, which was paradise on earth, into mortal life in a harsh world.

Adam and Eve are thought to be the first humans in all three of the world's major monotheistic religions—Judaism, Christianity, and Islam. Not all three believe in Original Sin, however.

PALM SUNDAY. The Sunday before Easter in the Christian calendar and the start of Holy Week. The name comes from the custom in some churches of carrying palm branches in a procession on that day. It marks the entry of Jesus into Jerusalem and refers to the palm-bearing crowds who greeted him there. *See also* EASTER and JESUS.

PARSEES. Another spelling of Parsis. *See also* PARSIS.

PARSIS. A religious group from the Bombay area of India. Parsis are members of the Zoroastrian religion. They fled to India from Persia in the eighth century A.D. to escape the Moslems. *See also* ZOROASTRIANISM.

PASSION OF CHRIST. The sufferings of Jesus on the cross or before his crucifixion. Passion music tells the Gospel story of Jesus' anguish. A dramatic performance that represents the suffering and death of Jesus is called a passion play. *See also* JESUS.

PASSOVER. One of the major religious festivals of the Jewish people.
    Passover is basically a spring celebration that became associated with the escape of the Jews from Egypt, where they were slaves 3,200 years ago.

Passover is also a reminder of other times when the Jews have triumphed over tyranny and oppression.

The name Passover (*Pesach* in Hebrew) comes from the last of ten plagues that God inflicted on Egypt when the pharaoh would not free the Jews. God sent an angel to kill the eldest son of each Egyptian household but told him to "pass over" the homes of the Israelites, whose doors were to be marked by the blood of a lamb.

Jews celebrate Passover with a ceremonial meal called the seder. The story of the Israelites' deliverance from Egypt is read aloud from a small book called the Haggadah. Everything that is eaten at the seder has a special meaning. Matzo, which is flat, or unleavened, bread, is a reminder of the flight from Egypt, when there was not enough time to let the dough rise. Haroset, a combination of apples and nuts, represents the mortar used by the Jews when they worked as slaves. Jews believe that the prophet Elijah will come on a Passover to announce the coming of the Messiah. During the seder a glass is filled with wine and the door opened for Elijah. *See also* JUDAISM and MOSES.

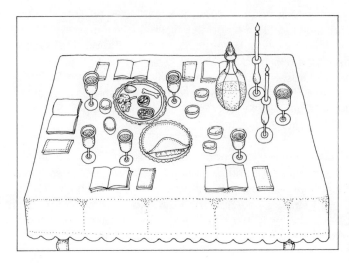

A Passover table

PAUL, SAINT. An organizer of the early Christian Church. Saint Paul was important in making converts and is credited with bringing Christianity to Europe.

PENTATEUCH. The first five books of the Hebrew Bible. Also called the Law or the Torah. *See also* BIBLE.

PENTECOST. An important spring feast for both Jews and Christians.

Pentecost means ''fifty'' in Greek. It is the Greek name of the Jewish feast of *Shavuot* that falls fifty days after Passover.

For Christians, Pentecost is the seventh Sunday after Easter. It occurs fifty days after the resurrection of Christ and marks the end of the Easter season. Christian tradition holds that on the day of Pentecost, the disciples received from the Holy Ghost the power to speak in many tongues. This allowed them to show more zeal in their work. The holiday is also called Whitsunday (White Sunday) in England. *See also* CHRISTIANITY; JUDAISM; and SHAVUOT.

PETER, SAINT. One of the twelve apostles. Jesus gave him the name *Peter*, which means ''rock.'' Roman Catholics believe that Jesus chose Peter to head his first church on earth. *See also* APOSTLES and POPE.

PILGRIMAGE. A journey to a sacred place of a particular religion. Ancient Greeks went on pilgrimages to Eleusis and Delphi. Hindus in India travel to the Ganges River and to the holy city of Banaras. Jews go to the Western Wall in Jerusalem. For Moslems, a pilgrimage to Mecca is part of their religion. Christians visit holy places in Jerusalem, Bethlehem, and Nazareth, as well as Rome and the Vatican. Roman Catholics also make pilgrimages to shrines at Lourdes in France, Guadalupe Hidalgo in Mexico, and Fátima in Portugal. *See also* MECCA and WESTERN WALL.

POLYTHEISM. The belief in more than one god. Polytheism originated among primitive peoples who identified the forces of nature with various supernatural powers. They assumed that different gods controlled the sun, moon, seasons, and so on. The ancient Greeks and Romans both had polytheistic forms of worship. Eventually, as one deity became more important than the others, polytheism gave way to monotheism, the worship of one God.

POPE. The head of the Roman Catholic Church as well as bishop of Rome. An almost unbroken line of nearly three hundred popes dates back to Saint Peter the Apostle, who is believed to have served from A.D. 42 to 67.

The pope governs from Vatican City, a tiny independent state of 108 acres entirely within the city of Rome. His home church is St. Peter's.

Any Roman Catholic can be elected pope. Since the 1300s, however, the pope has always been chosen from among the cardinals. From the 1500s until today he has also been Italian. The exception is the current pope, Pope John Paul II (elected in 1978), who is Polish.

The power of the pope over spiritual matters of the Catholic Church is absolute. The pope also has full control of the political administration of the Vatican. Any religious statement or ruling he makes is considered infallible, that is, without error. *See also* CARDINAL and VATICAN.

PRAYER. A form of worship directed to God or the Supreme Being of a religion. Among the many types of prayer are those that show devotion to the deity, seek divine help, offer thanks, or confess misdeeds.

PREDESTINATION. Generally, the belief that whatever happens during a person's lifetime is predetermined, or decided in advance, by God. Almost all religions believe in some form of predetermination.

Predestination also refers specifically to the Protestant Calvinist doctrine that says that certain people are elected at birth by God for salvation. *See also* CALVIN, JOHN.

PRESBYTERIANS. One of the denominations of Protestantism. Presbyterians follow the teachings of John Calvin, who believed that God should be worshiped in a simple and dignified way. Calvin also emphasized the principle of predestination and the importance of the individual in God's eyes.

The Presbyterian Church developed from the Reformed Church that Calvin had organized in Switzerland in the 1500s and from John Knox's Reformed Church of Scotland.

Each church is led by a minister and a board of elders. The word *presbyterian* comes from the Greek word for elder. There are close to 1 million Presbyterians in the United States today. *See also* CALVIN, JOHN; PREDESTINATION; and PROTESTANTISM.

PRIEST. A member of the clergy who leads religious services. Although the spiritual leaders of the ancient Jews were called priests, today they are known as rabbis. Most of the Christian churches, including the Roman Catholic, Anglican, Episcopal, Mormon, Eastern Orthodox, and some Lutheran churches have priests. Members of the clergy in Buddhism and Shintoism are also called priests.

PROPHET. Someone who is thought to speak for God or by divine inspiration. Moses is considered one of the greatest prophets in Judaism. The prophet Mohammed taught the faith of Islam. The word comes from the Greek and means "one who proclaims."

PROTESTANTISM. The various Christian churches, other than the Roman Catholic or Eastern Orthodox, that grew from the Protestant Reformation of the sixteenth century.

Protestants belong to hundreds of different churches. Each one has somewhat different beliefs and forms of worship. Most share a number of common doctrines. Protestants do not accept the authority of the pope but consider the Bible to be the final spiritual authority. Every individual is responsible directly to God and not to the church. And all members of the congregation take part in ritual worship.

About 340 million people belong to Protestant churches worldwide. Most live in Europe and North America. *See also* BAPTISTS; CALVIN, JOHN; CHURCH OF ENGLAND; EPISCOPALIANS; FRIENDS, SOCIETY OF; JEHOVAH'S WITNESSES; LUTHERANS; MENNONITES; METHODISTS; MORMONS; PRESBYTERIANS; PURITANS; REFORMATION; SEVENTH-DAY ADVENTISTS; and UNITARIANS.

PROTESTANT REFORMATION. *See* REFORMATION.

PSALMS. The name of one of the books in the Old Testament. Psalms contains about 150 religious Hebrew hymnlike poems. Tradition holds that some were written by King David. Many have been set to music.

Hymns are used in both Jewish and Christian worship. The most oft-recited psalm is probably the twenty-third, which starts, "The Lord is my Shepherd, I shall not want." *See also* BIBLE.

PURGATORY. A state after death, according to Roman Catholic belief, in which the departed must pay for their sins before entering heaven. Catholics believe that these sufferings are not as bad as those in hell because they do not last forever, and they can be lessened by the prayers of family or friends.

PURIM. A spring festival celebrated by Jews on the fourteenth day of Adar in the Hebrew calendar. Purim marks Queen Esther's fabled saving of the Jews in

Persia (now Iran) from a massacre ordered by the wicked Haman, prime minister to King Ahasuerus. The name probably comes from the Hebrew word for lot (as in lottery). Lots had been drawn to decide on a day for the massacre. The story of Purim can be found in the Bible in the Book of Esther.

Some Jews fast on the day preceding Purim because it was said that Esther fasted before pleading with Ahasuerus. Mostly the holiday is joyous. People eat *hamentashen,* little cakes in the shape of Haman's three-cornered hat, and use noisemakers to drown out the sound of Haman's name every time it is mentioned.

PURITANS. Originally a term for a reform group of the Church of England in the sixteenth century. The Puritans were so-called because they wanted to purify and simplify church practices and impose stricter moral standards on the people.

The Puritans, wanting the right to worship as they wished, left England and journeyed to the New World aboard the *Mayflower.* While still on the ship, they signed the Mayflower Compact, a set of laws that would establish certain concepts of religious freedom in America. The painting is by Robert W. Weir.

**John Calvin,
1509–1564**

The Puritans followed many of the principles of John Calvin, one of the leaders of the Protestant Reformation. They were against elaborate rituals and the use of music at church services. They believed in religious tolerance and freedom of the individual to worship in his or her own way.

The so-called Puritan ethic calls for rigorous self-examination. It calls for hard work as a spiritual exercise and also promotes the idea that those of the "elect" who labor hard will be rewarded in life as well as after death.

A group of Puritans came to America in 1620 and founded the Massachusetts Bay Colony. They played a large role in American history in establishing the idea of religious freedom and the economic system of capitalism. Today, the term *puritan* refers to one who is very strict in religious and moral matters. *See also* CALVIN, JOHN; and PREDESTINATION.

Q

QUAKER. A member of the Society of Friends, although members of the society generally do not use the term. *See also* FRIENDS, SOCIETY OF.

A Quaker meeting

RABBI. An ordained spiritual leader of a Jewish congregation. The word comes from the Hebrew and means either "my teacher" or "my master." Rabbis receive their training at seminaries. Women may serve as rabbis in the Reform and Conservative branches of Judaism. The rabbi leads services, conducts weddings and funerals, cares for the spiritual lives of congregation members, and directs religious education in the community. *See also* JUDAISM.

RAMADAN. The ninth month of the year in the Islamic calendar. During this month all Moslems, except for the sick, must fast from dawn until sunset. Ramadan commemorates the first revelation of the Koran. *See also* KORAN and ISLAM.

RAMAYANA. Hindu epic poem from India, composed around the first or second century B.C. The poem tells the story of Rama, who was a human incarnation of the god Vishnu. *See also* HINDUISM and VISHNU.

REFORMATION. The religious movement of the sixteenth century that led to a schism, or split, in the Christian Church and to the establishment of Protestantism.

The Reformation sprang from a number of different causes. The renaissance brought with it growth in learning, a new belief in the value and dignity of the individual, and a general questioning of Church authority. Powerful monarchs took control of vast lands as the old feudal system broke down. The abuses and corruption of much of the leadership of the Roman Catholic Church was becoming intolerable to many.

Martin Luther, a German Catholic monk, was one of the leading figures of the Reformation. In 1517 he nailed his Ninety-five Theses on the Castle Church door in Wittenberg. It listed some of the abuses he found in the Catholic Church.

Luther hoped by this to stir debate within the Church; he expected the pope to bring about reform once he had been made aware of the problems. But his criticisms led to very strong anti-Church feelings and to the formation of a new religious body, the Lutheran Church. The Lutheran group became the first Protestant denomination.

The Lutherans lived in Germany. But Switzerland, France, Great Britain, and Scandanavia had similar movements. Protestant churches formed in all of these areas during the sixteenth century. *See also* LUTHER, MARTIN; and PROTESTANTISM.

REINCARNATION. The religious belief that after a person's death, his or her soul enters a new body. Reincarnation is a doctrine found most notably in the Buddhist, Jain, and Hindu religions. *See also* HINDUISM and IMMORTALITY.

RESURRECTION. The return of the dead to a living state. According to the Gospels, Jesus arose from his tomb three days after he was crucified. Mary Magdalene went to his burial place and found it empty. An angel told her that Jesus had been resurrected. The Gospels say he appeared to his disciples, taught them for forty days, and then ascended to heaven. The rising again, or resurrection, of the dead on Judgment Day is a part of both Judaism and Christianity. *See also* EASTER and JESUS.

RITE. A prescribed or customary act in religious observance. Many religious rites are connected to major events or changes in a person's life, such as birth, marriage, and death.

RITUAL. An established system of rites that involves the use of symbols and ceremonies. The symbols serve as reminders of religious ideas. In Buddhism, for example, the Wheel of Law symbolizes the path to enlightenment; in Christianity, the cross represents salvation through Christ's crucifixion. Customs and ceremonies that are part of religion help people express their beliefs and also act as a way to connect the faithful with the divine force they believe in. Many Hindus, for example, make offerings to statues of local deities. Moslems face east, toward Mecca, when they pray.

ROMAN CATHOLICISM. The Christian Church headed by the pope. Roman Catholics trace their history back to Saint Peter, who is considered to have been the first pope of the Church of Rome.

This painting of the crucifixion of Jesus is by artist Bernardo Daddi.

Roman Catholics believe in one God and in the writings of the Christian Bible. They believe that people can communicate with God through prayer and achieve eternal life through the death of Jesus. Catholic theology also accepts salvation through good works. The Church requires a number of rites of worship. The Eucharist, or Communion, is of primary importance.

The pope in Rome is the spiritual head of the Roman Catholic Church. His word is believed to be infallible, that is, without error. Under him are the cardinals, who make up the Sacred College. Roman Catholic churches around the world are administered by a number of archbishops and bishops. The spiritual leaders of the individual places of worship are priests. All Church leaders must be unmarried.

The Roman Catholic Church grew from the ministry of Jesus. In the time of Jesus and for many centuries following, the ruling Romans opposed him and persecuted his disciples.

In A.D. 876, a split developed within the Church that later led to the formation of a separate church, the Eastern Orthodox Church. In the 1500s, the Reformation resulted in the formation of a number of Protestant churches.

The Roman Catholic Church today has the largest number of Christian followers in the world. There are nearly 600 million Catholics worldwide, with about 133 million in the United States. The term *Catholic* was originally used for the Christian Church to suggest its universal nature. *See also* ARCHBISHOP; BISHOP; CHRISTIANITY; COMMUNION; POPE; PRIEST; and REFORMATION.

ROSARY. A string of beads made of wood, metal, or stone and used in praying. The rosary in the Roman Catholic Church has a circle of fifty small beads divided into equal sections by four large beads. A crucifix hangs from the rosary. Prayers to the Virgin Mary are said on the small beads. On one of the large beads the Lord's Prayer is recited; and on the crucifix the Apostles' Creed is said. Buddhists and Moslems also make use of beads in prayer. *See also* LORD'S PRAYER.

ROSH HASHANAH. The Jewish New Year celebration when Jews pray for forgiveness and long life. Rosh Hashanah is the start of ten days of penitence and prayer that ends on Yom Kippur, the Day of Atonement. *See also* YOM KIPPUR.

RUSSELL, CHARLES TAZE (1852–1916). Pennsylvania-born founder of Jehovah's Witnesses in 1881. *See also* JEHOVAH'S WITNESSES.

S

SABBATH. The Jewish day of rest. The Sabbath starts on Friday at sundown and ends at sunset on Saturday. Observant Jews celebrate the Sabbath with special food, song, and rest from work. Also, Orthodox Jews do not travel, use the telephone, write, or touch money. The rules to follow in observing the Sabbath are described in the Hebrew Bible, starting with the Ten Commandments. Some Christian sects also observe Saturday as the Sabbath.

The Sabbath evening is a family occasion. The woman of the house lights the traditional candles and recites the blessing. The man says a prayer, blesses the wine and bread, and slices the Sabbath loaf.

Many families attend synagogue after dinner. Often, the communal worship in the sanctuary is followed by a social hour in the temple's meeting hall.

SACRAMENT. A sacred ceremony of the Christian Church. The sacrament is a symbol of reaching a state of grace, or receiving spiritual benefit from Christ.

There are seven sacraments in the Roman Catholic and Eastern Orthodox churches: Eucharist, Baptism, Confirmation, Penance, Extreme Unction (or Anointing of the Sick), Matrimony, and Taking Holy Orders. Most Protestant churches have only two sacraments, Baptism and Eucharist. *See also* BAPTISM and COMMUNION.

SAINT. A person of great holiness, virtue, or benevolence who is declared by the Christian Church as having attained an exalted position in heaven and is thereby entitled to be venerated on earth. Reverence of saints is especially important in the Roman Catholic, Eastern Orthodox, and Anglican religions.

SALVATION. The religious doctrine of deliverance from the penalty of sin. Christianity teaches that salvation leads to eternal life, which is often described as a state of eternal bliss called heaven. If not saved, the soul may enter purgatory for cleansing or a state of eternal punishment called hell. Christians believe that salvation comes when individuals free themselves from sin with the help of Christ the Savior. Salvation is also part of Judaism and Islam. *See also* HELL; PREDESTINATION; and PURGATORY.

SALVATION ARMY. A Christian group, started in 1865 in England, to spread the word of Jesus and to help the poor and the needy. The founder, William Booth, was a Methodist minister. He began his work by holding religious meetings outdoors, in tents and theaters, and preaching anyplace he could draw a crowd.

In 1878, the movement was organized into a military structure. The members called it the Salvation Army and named William Booth their first general. In 1880, the Salvation Army began operating in the United States.

Today, the Salvation Army makes use of outdoor brass bands to attract passersby. Once the people are assembled, either a meeting is held on the street or everyone is invited indoors for a religious service.

Besides their spiritual work, the Salvation Army maintains hospitals, shelters for the homeless, and workshops to help those without jobs. There are about 500,000 members of the Salvation Army living in the United States today.

SEVENTH-DAY ADVENTISTS. Members of a conservative Protestant sect. The doctrine of the Seventh-day Adventist Church grew from the teachings of William Miller (1782–1849), who predicted the end of the world in 1843 on the basis of his reading of the biblical Book of Daniel. He later revised the date to October 22, 1844.

When the end did not occur, Miller's followers affirmed their belief that Christ would again appear on earth but at some time in the future. They stressed the importance of keeping Saturday, the seventh day of the week, as a holy day. In May 1863, a new formal church was organized to carry on these beliefs; it was named the Seventh-day Adventist Church. About 600,000 members live in the United States today.

SHAVUOT. A religious festival of the Jewish people. The holiday comes fifty days after Passover. The Hebrew Bible calls it the Feast of Weeks or the Feast of First Fruits. The celebration marks the grain harvest and the time when the ancients brought their first fruits to Mount Zion. According to tradition, Moses received the Torah from God on this day. It is customary to decorate homes and synagogues with flowers on Shavuot. Some observant Jews study the Torah the entire night before the feast. *See also* JUDAISM; PENTECOST; and TORAH.

SHINTO. The native religion of Japan. *Shinto* means "way of the higher spirits." The religion consists mostly of nature and ancestor worship. Shintoists believe that spirits can influence events and affect people's lives.

Old Shinto was the religion of Japan until A.D. 552, when Buddhism was brought in from China. For most of Japan's history, Shinto has existed alongside Buddhism and, later, Confucianism and Taoism. Shinto as an official religion was revived during the reigns of the Tokugawa rulers, from 1603 to 1867.

In 1882 the government of Japan divided the religion into Sect Shinto and State Shinto. The former focused on religious faith. The latter was more concerned with history and patriotism.

In time, though, State Shinto became a state religion. The Japanese constitution of 1889 granted religious liberty, but State Shinto was officially approved to help protect Japan from growing Western influence. Conservatives revived the Old Shinto myth of the emperor's descent from the sun goddess.

When the Americans occupied Japan, just after World War II, however, they abolished State Shinto as a state religion, and the emperor was forced to publicly deny his divinity. Today, the practice of Sect Shinto continues in Japan. About 57 million Japanese currently follow Shintoism.

At home, a Shintoist worships before a *Kami-dana*, or "spiritshelf." The altar contains the names of the family's protective spirits and a small lamp. Family members may place the first rice cooked each day or rice wine on the shelf in homage to the spirits. On All Souls' Day, also called the Festival of the Lanterns, the shrines of the ancestors are decorated, and lanterns are lit in the streets to lead the spirits inside.

Shintoists also pray at public shrines dedicated to their favorite gods or spirits. They thank the spirit and make offerings to it of rice or money. Each shrine is approached through a *torii*, or gateway, that symbolizes the passage from everyday life to a sacred place.

SIKHISM. A religion that combines some Hindu and some Islamic beliefs. Tradition holds that Sikhism was founded by Nanak (1469–1539), a guru or teacher in India who received divine revelation. The Sikhs believe in one God, called *Nam*, meaning "the Name."

In the Sikh religion God is worshiped in temples, but Sikh temples contain no images of Nam. The Sikh holy book is the Adi Granth. Services in the temples include prayers, readings from the sacred book, and offerings made to Nam. Worshipers often share a meal after the service.

SIVA. The god who is known as the Destroyer in the Hindu religion. The two other Hindu gods are Brahma the Creator and Vishnu the Preserver. The three gods are different aspects of the Supreme Being, Brahman.

The name *Siva* means "kind" or "favorable." Although the god can seem frightening and evil, followers of Siva believe that he destroys in order to make way for the new. They further believe that Siva restores what is destroyed. This makes possible the continuation and endless renewal of the universe. Siva is also known and worshiped in the person of his wife, who has many names, including Kali ("the Black") and Parvati ("the Maintainer"), and who also has powers over life and death. *See also* HINDUISM.

SMITH, JOSEPH (1805–1844). The American religious leader who founded the Church of Jesus Christ of the Latter-Day Saints. *See also* MORMONS.

SMYTH, JOHN. *See* BAPTISTS.

SOLOMON. The king of Israel and son of David and Bathsheba, who lived around the tenth century B.C. Solomon, noted for his wealth and great wisdom, built a magnificent temple in Jerusalem. Under his rule, Israel reached its greatest heights in prosperity and glory.

SPANISH INQUISITION. The term refers to the Inquisition in Spain, which was under state control and lasted from 1480 until 1834. The punishment of Christian heretics (nonbelievers) and such non-Christians as Jews and Moslems was especially severe in the sixteenth century, and included torture, imprisonment, and death. *See also* INQUISITION.

SPIRITUALISM. A religious philosophy that emphasizes the spiritual rather than the material or temporal. Some spiritualists are of the opinion that only the spirit is real, and that matter exists only in the mind.

SUFISM. The beliefs of a mystic sect of Moslems called Sufis. The word *Sufi*, which comes from the Arabic, means "man of wool." Sufism has inspired a large body of symbolic religious poetry.

SUPERNATURALISM. A belief in beings and events that do not fit the known laws of nature. People who accept on faith that God exists as a being or who believe in miracles are supernaturalists. They say that neither the existence of a divine figure nor miracles can be explained as natural events.

SYNAGOGUE. A building where Jews gather for worship. The word comes from the Greek word for assembly.

The first synagogues probably appeared after the Jews were exiled from Babylonia in the 500s B.C. and found themselves in a foreign land where they had no central temple in which to worship. Later, in the year A.D. 79, the Romans destroyed the great temple in Jerusalem, the center of their faith. The Jews were then widely scattered around the world and proceeded to set up synagogues in foreign lands as centers of Jewish religious life. These synagogues were also used as courts of law and places of study. Many consider the synagogues responsible for preserving Judaism.

The rolls of scripture, the Torah, are kept in a chest known as the Holy Ark at the front of the synagogue's sanctuary. A lamp burns there all the time. The eternal light symbolizes the continuing presence of God. Various members of the congregation are called on to read from the Torah during prayer services, which are led by a rabbi. In Orthodox synagogues men sit on one side of a screen and women on the other.

The oldest synagogue in existence in the United States today is the Touro Synagogue in Newport, Rhode Island. It dates from 1763. *See also* JUDAISM and RABBI.

TABERNACLE. According to the Hebrew Bible, the Israelites built the Tabernacle, a portable sanctuary, as a place of worship during their wanderings in the desert. A Jewish festival called Sukkoth is also known as the Feast of the Tabernacles.

The famous Mormon Tabernacle is in Salt Lake City.

TALMUD. An interpretation and adaptation of the original Torah. The Talmud is second in importance to the Torah, or Pentateuch, which is the first five books of the Hebrew Bible.

The Talmud is divided into two parts, the Mishna (in Hebrew) and the Gemara (in Aramaic). The sixty-three separate books of the Mishna contain the laws. The Gemara has thirty-six books of commentaries on the laws.

Two different versions of the Talmud were produced, one in Jerusalem in the fifth century A.D. and the other in Babylon in the sixth century A.D. The Babylonian Talmud is the one that survived and is used today. *See also* BIBLE and TORAH.

TAOISM. A popular religion of China that derives from the philosophy of Lao-tzu, who is believed to have lived in the seventh century B.C., around the same time as Confucius, although the date is disputed.

The term *Tao* means "the Way." Taoism encourages a life of moderation and the avoidance of extremes of any kind. Happiness lies in living in harmony with nature, trying not to change anything by force. Passivity and conforming to the natural course of events are considered virtues.

Lao-tzu's teachings were added to by Chwang-tzu, a follower who was a brilliant writer and lived about two hundred years after the master. The book *Tao Te Ching* was probably written in the third century B.C. It contains much of the doctrine of the religion. Taoism as an organized religion dates from the first century A.D. In recent times, it has declined somewhat in popularity. There are about 31 million Taoists today, almost all among the peasants of China. *See also* LAO-TZU.

TEN COMMANDMENTS. The divine law that, according to tradition, was given by God to Moses on Mount Sinai and delivered by Moses to the Israelites.

The Ten Commandments

The Ten Commandments are at the heart of the teachings of Christianity and Islam as well as Judaism. They are: (1) Thou shalt have no other gods before Me. (2) Thou shalt not make unto thee any graven image. (3) Thou shalt not take the name of the Lord thy God in vain. (4) Thou shalt remember the Sabbath Day, to keep it holy. (5) Thou shalt honor thy father and thy mother. (6) Thou shalt not kill. (7) Thou shalt not commit adultery. (8) Thou shalt not steal. (9) Thou shalt not bear false witness against thy neighbor. (10) Thou shalt not covet thy neighbor's house.

THEISM. The belief in, or the belief in the existence of, one or more gods. Theism is opposed in meaning to atheism.

THEOLOGY. The study of one or many gods and religious questions. Theology investigates the relationship between the divine and human and compares the doctrines of the various religions.

TORAH. The first five books of the Hebrew Bible. Other names for the Torah are the Law and the Pentateuch. *See also* BIBLE.

TRANSUBSTANTIATION. The belief in the Roman Catholic Church that the bread and wine used in Communion are changed into the body and blood of Jesus during the ceremony, although they keep the appearance of bread and wine. *See also* COMMUNION.

TRINITY. The Christian belief that God exists in three persons which, although distinct, form one Godhead. These persons are God the Father, God the Son (or Jesus), and God the Holy Ghost. The Trinity was defined at the First Council of Nicaea in A.D. 325, following much controversy over relationships within it.

Most Christians consider the Trinity a mystery that can never be fully understood by humans. Sometimes the three persons that make up the Trinity are thought of as a single entity, with three aspects. The traditional belief, though, is that God the Father is the Creator, God the Son is the Saver of Souls, and God the Holy Ghost gives the gift of sanctification, or holiness. It is generally accepted that each one shares fully in the activities of the others. *See also* CHRISTIANITY.

UNITARIANS. Members of one of the more liberal Christian churches. The name comes from the Unitarians' acceptance of God as a single being, rather than believing in the doctrine of the Trinity. Unitarians have no creed other than the statement, "In the love of truth, and in the spirit of Jesus, we unite for the worship of God and the service of man." The Church, however, does not require its members to confess belief in this or any other creed or doctrine.

The main ideas of the Unitarian Church have been accepted by some since the days of the Reformation. The Church was formally organized, though, in 1825.

In 1961, the Universalist Church joined the Unitarians, creating the Unitarian Universalist Association. About 140,000 Unitarians live in the United States today.

UPANISHADS. A set of sacred writings of ancient Hinduism. The Upanishads date from about the seventh to the fourth centuries B.C. They set forth in philosophical terms the concept of Brahman, the Supreme Being or World Spirit, in the Hindu religion.

They also emphasize direct knowledge of Brahman and true understanding of ourselves as the means of reaching a state of bliss. *See also* BRAHMAN; HINDUISM; and YOGA.

VATICAN. Home of the pope, the head of the Roman Catholic Church. Vatican City, which consists of 108 acres within the city of Rome, Italy, is the smallest independent country in the world. The pope is absolute ruler of Vatican City.

Within the Vatican is St. Peter's Church, the largest Christian church in the world. There is also Vatican Palace, several connected buildings that contain over a thousand rooms, including the pope's apartment and some of the offices for the administration of the Roman Catholic Church. Many priceless art treasures are contained within the Vatican Museum. The famed Sistine Chapel, with its ceiling and wall paintings by Michelangelo, is located here. Other Vatican buildings house the library and archive.

The Vatican is protected by the Swiss Guard. In their bright yellow, orange, and blue uniforms they protect the pope and serve as guards and watchmen. *See also* POPE and ROMAN CATHOLICISM.

VEDAS. The oldest and most sacred scriptures of Hinduism. The word means "knowledge" or "body of knowledge."

The Vedas date from about 1500 B.C.. They are written in Sanskrit. Included are over a thousand hymns to a number of gods, prayers to accompany sacrifices, chants, spells, and incantations. They later came to include religious writings called the Brahmanas, which contain directions for the proper ritual use of the hymns and prayers of the Vedas.

There are four Vedas, of which the Rig Veda is the oldest and most important. Many Hindus believe it was created before the world began. While many of the traditions and rituals in the Vedas have been given up, some of the basic beliefs continue to this day. *See also* HINDUISM.

VIRGIN MARY. The title given to the mother of Jesus. According to tradition, Mary gave birth to Jesus in a stable in Bethlehem. She had come there, it is told, from her home in Nazareth with her husband, Joseph, to be counted in the census. Little is known of her life after the death of Jesus. She is thought by some to have died in Jerusalem in the year A.D. 63.

The Virgin Mary is greatly honored by the Roman Catholic and Eastern Orthodox churches. Principal feasts dedicated to her are Immaculate Conception (December 8), Annunciation (March 25), and Assumption (August 15).

Over the years a number of people have reported seeing visions of the Virgin Mary. The best-known appearances occurred in 1531 at Guadalupe Hidalgo, Mexico; in 1830 in Paris; in 1858 at Lourdes, France; and in 1917 at Fátima, Portugal. *See also* ANNUNCIATION; IMMACULATE CONCEPTION; and JESUS.

VISHNU. The World Preserver in the Hindu religion. Vishnu is the second of the

In Hindu mythology, Vishnu is often described as resting on a many-headed cobra floating in an ocean of milk. The ocean may represent totality and peace, the serpent eternity. Vishnu's wife, Lakshmi, goddess of harmony and plenty, attends him. The lotus-flower coming from Vishnu's navel holds Brahma, the Creator of the Universe.

three aspects of Brahman, which includes Brahma, Vishnu, and Siva. Followers of Vishnu are called Vishnuites.

According to Hindu teachings, Vishnu, in order to overcome evil, expressed his will to the world through ten rebirths, or incarnations. Three of the most important are Rama, the ideal man; Krishna, the loved hero; and Buddha, the prophet. Nirvana, Hindus believe, is to be obtained primarily through a life of faith and devotion to one of the deities.

The epic poem *Ramayana* relates the adventures of the brave Rama and his rescue of his wife Sita from evil. Included in the Mahabharata, one of the holy books of the Vishnuites, are accounts of Krishna, the chariot driver of Prince Arjuna, and explanations of Krishna's doctrine. *See also* KRISHNA; HINDUISM; and RAMAYANA.

W-Y

WESLEY, JOHN (1703–1791). Founder of Methodism, one of the sects of Protestantism. John Wesley was born in England and became a minister of the Church of England while studying at Oxford University.

In 1735, Wesley came as a missionary to Georgia in the American colonies. He returned to England in 1738 and in that same year had a religious experience that convinced him that salvation could be obtained only through faith in Jesus.

This belief became the central theme of his preaching. He traveled widely, bringing his message to the people at open-air meetings instead of expecting them to come to church. Out of all this activity a new sect emerged in 1784, the Methodist Church. *See also* METHODISM and SALVATION.

YOGA. A technique of mental and physical discipline within the Hindu religion. Yoga consists of a system of exercises that the individual follows to gain control over mind and body. It offers precise directions for slowing down bodily activity and controlling posture, breathing, and thought. The aim is to free oneself from the material world and thereby achieve union of the self with Brahman, the Supreme Being. The word is from the Sanskrit and means "union." A person who practices yoga to attain union with Brahman is a yogi or yogin. The techniques of yoga are contained in the Upanishads. *See also* HINDUISM and UPANISHADS.

Some Yoga Postures

The Plough

The Half-Lotus

The Cobra

The Locust

YOM KIPPUR. The most holy day of the Jewish calendar. Yom Kippur is also called the Day of Atonement. The holiday always falls at the end of September or beginning of October, ten days after the Jewish New Year.

Jews observe the day with a twenty-four-hour fast, from sundown on the eve of the holiday to sundown on Yom Kippur. Yom Kippur is a time to confess sins committed during the year and pray for forgiveness. It is also an occasion to remember the dead and to forget quarrels. At the end of the day, which many spend in synagogue reciting prayers, the shofar, a huge ram's horn trumpet, is blown. Jews then return home to break the fast with a light meal.

YOUNG, BRIGHAM (1801–1877). The second president of the Church of Jesus Christ of Latter-Day Saints. In 1846, Young led the members of his church, called Mormons, from their homes in Illinois to Salt Lake Valley, Utah. In 1847 he was elected head of the Mormons, replacing the founder, Joseph Smith, who was murdered in 1844. He was also appointed the first governor of the Territory of Utah. Many non-Mormons opposed him, though, because he followed the Mormon practice of polygamy and had twenty-seven wives. *See also* MORMONS.

Brigham Young, 1801–1877

Z

ZARATHUSTRA. *See* ZOROASTER.

ZEN. A Chinese and Japanese sect of Mayahana Buddhism. The major belief of Zen is that only through self-knowledge and understanding obtained through meditation can a person experience the oneness of all reality.

There is little formal instruction in Zen Buddhism. Typically, the master says, "My words are mine and not yours, and do not belong to you. All must come out of your own being."

The master asks riddles that have no answers; these are called *koans*. He also leads nonsensical discussions, called *mondos*. The riddles and questions have nothing to do with religion. Rather, they challenge the pupil to go beyond intellect or reason in order to achieve enlightenment. Some typical *koans* are: What was your face like before you were born? What is the sound of one hand clapping?

A typical *mondo* dialogue is:

Pupil: What is Buddha?
Master: The cat climbs the post.
Pupil: I don't understand.
Master: Then ask the post.

Zen originated in China during the sixth century A.D. Bodhidharma, who is said to have been an Indian scholar, was its founder. In Chinese this school of Buddhism is called Ch'an.

Zen flourished in China until the Ming dynasty (1368–1622) and then began to fade. A new burst of interest in Zen developed in Japan after World War II. It is still very strong there, with an estimated 5 million Zen Buddhists in Japan today.

ZOROASTER (660–583 B.C.). Religious leader born in ancient Persia (now Iran), who founded the Zoroastrian religion. He is also known as Zarathustra.

Through a series of visions he had from age thirty to forty, Zoroaster conceived a new religion. At first he was unable to win any converts. But eventually he gained the support of King Vishtaspa, and the religion spread. Worldwide, there are about 300,000 Zoroastrians today. *See also* ZOROASTRIANISM.

ZOROASTRIANISM. A religion founded in Persia (now Iran) around the year 600 B.C. by Zoroaster. The sacred book of the religion is the Zend-Avesta. Among its teachings is the belief that there is only one God, Ahura Mazda, who was later renamed Ormazd. In time, worship of the forces of nature became part of the religion. Also, the doctrine that all souls would be saved was added. Good people would go right to paradise after death; the wicked would first be purified in hell, then enter heaven.

Only about 11,000 adherents of Zoroastrianism remain in Iran today. The Parsis (or Parsees) of India, who number around 100,000, are members of a Zoroastrian sect. *See also* PARSIS and ZOROASTER.